The Golden Understanding

Roy Norvill was born in 1926 in South London.
He began work as an electrician's apprentice, but at 17 decided to become a professional drummer and arranger.
From 1952 he toured as a freelance musician, playing jazz and accompanying a variety of artists.
He undertook extensive research which led to the discovery of an alternative philosophy of religion, mysticism and the occult. zz
In 1980, forsaking touring, he settled in Brighton to set down this discovery in detail, producing the trilogy, *Hermes Unveiled, The Language of the Gods*, and now *The Golden Understanding*.
He is still active as a drummer and arranger.

ROY NORVILL

The Golden Understanding

ASHGROVE PRESS, BATH

First published in Great Britain by
ASHGROVE PRESS LIMITED
4 Brassmill Centre, Brassmill Lane,
Bath, Avon, BA1 3JN

and distributed in the USA by
Avery Publishing Group Inc.
120 Old Broadway
Garden City Park
New York 11040.

First published 1989

British Library Cataloguing in Publication Data

Norvill, Roy
  The Golden Understanding
  1. Hermeticism
  1. Title
  299. '93

        ISBN 1–85398–011–0

Photoset by Ann Buchan (Typesetters)
Middlesex
Printed and bound by Billings,
Worcester

Contents

Introduction 9

Chapter One 15

Chapter Two 27

Chapter Three 48

Chapter Four 66

Chapter Five 84

Chapter Six 104

Chapter Seven 122

Chapter Eight 137

Chapter Nine 152

Chapter Ten 166

Conclusion 177

Appendix: The Turin Shroud 179

Bibliography 189

Front cover engraving;   Its symbolism defined.

The scene depicts a *shepherd* who has *wandered away from his usual path* to *climb a mount*. *Young and beardless,* he *wears a cap* and carries a *crook* with which to *guide his sheep*. Although *rocky*, the mount is also a *garden*, or a *grotto*, in the *centre* of which stands a *tree* (the *Persea*, the *Sycamore* or the *Oak*). From the height a village and a *lake* can be seen. *Kneeling* (a sign of *humility*) the shepherd has *found a way* to peer into a world that is *normally hidden from view*. Note that only the shepherd's *head* and *right hand* penetrate the hidden dimension, whilst the *left hand* remains in the normal world, holding the crook which was used to make the hole. It is just after *dawn*, for although the *Moon* and *stars* are present, the *Sun*, with its *seven rays*, is shown low in the sky, having *not long risen*. The hidden dimension itself is like *nothing known to mankind*, showing impossible possibilities, such as a *wheel turning in upon itself.*

(Note: Exposition of the key words emphasised in the above are given in *Hermes Unveiled* and *The Language of the Gods*.)

Introduction

Early this century, American author Manly P. Hall produced what many consider to be the ultimate encyclopeadia of Rosicrucian philosophy, his *Masonic, Hermetic, Cabbalistic & Rosicrucian Symbolical Philosophy*. In a chapter dealing with cyphers and codes, he analyses various methods of transmiting secret messages, coming at last to what he terms the Acroamatic (a word meaning 'esoteric', but seldom found in modern dictionaries). Of this particular form, he wrote:

> The religious and philosophical writings of all nations abound with acroamatic cryptograms, that is, parables and allegories. The acroamatic is unique in that the document containing it may be translated or reprinted without affecting the cryptogram. Parables and allegories have been used since remote antiquity to present moral truths in an attractive and understandable manner. The acroamatic cryptogram is a pictorial cypher in words and its symbolism must be so interpreted. The Old and New Testaments of the Jews, the writings of Plato and Aristotle, Homer's *Odyssey* and *Iliad*, Virgil's *Aeneid*, the *Metamorphosis* of Apuleius, and *Aesop's Fables* are outstanding examples of acroamatic cryptography in which are concealed the deepest and most sublime truths of ancient mystical philosophy.

As might be expected of a philosopher in possession of the highest knowledge, Manly P. Hall offered no explanation of precisely how such parables and allegories could be interpreted in the correct manner. Following a tradition established over the preceeding five thousand years or more, he *remained silent*, leaving his readers to speculate on their own account, or to doubt if such a secret code did actually exist. Not unexpectedly, the idea that ordinary words and phrases can be utilised in so subtle and innocuous a manner as to require a specially developed sense of intuition in order to extract the hidden intent remains for most beyond the bounds of credibility. Yet incontestible proof that such a contrived code does exist was given openly in the late 19th century by the Benedictine monk, Dom Antoine-Joseph Pernety, in his work *A Treatise On The Great Art*. Therein the author devoted many pages to a strange listing of names, words and phrases which, he claimed, concealed the secret Hermetic way to the Philosophers' Stone. The deep significance of this disclosure, in all likelihood the first of its kind, was never wholly appreciated by the public at large, for Pernety, in fear of certain vilification, did not dare to apply his code words to the enciphered texts.

Since Pernety's day, however, tremendous sociological and psychological changes have been wrought. Concepts have broadened out of all recognition, many fallacies have been swept aside, and it is no longer imperative to suppress knowledge for the benefit of a few institutions who are jealous of their stranglehold on the public imagination.

With the publication of *Hermes Unveiled* (1986) and *The Language Of The Gods* (1987), therefore, a comprehensive exposition of the code was at long last made available to all, the texts exemplifying in great detail its application to documents of historical, religious, philosophical and mystical content on the one hand, and to fiction, fantasy and folklore on the other.

It would be reasonable to suggest that the only likely casualty of this exercise would have been the strict ideology of the religious Fundamentalist – those who believe implicitly in the literal word of their Scripture. The revelation of a secret message enshrined in the pages of *She* would cause no trepidation to H. Rider Haggard devotees, merely curiosity, for the extraction of a second meaning from the text would not alter the reader's knowledge that the outward story was pure fiction. But to show that the same allegorical manipulation was employed by those who drafted the four Gospels may have alarmed Fundamentalists, for it implies that the literal meaning of the Jesus story is of very minor importance indeed compared to the concealed message and, what is worse, that the story needed to be fiction in order to carry the inner message successfully. I feel certain, however, that any such alarm would have been on a small scale, for seventeen hundred years of intense indoctrination is not easily set to one side, in spite of the fact that the question has been raised on several previous occasions. David Friedrich Strauss, a scholar of 19th century Germany, who held a position at the Tubingen Protestant seminary, is a case which springs to mind. An avid devotee of the Hegelian philosophical system, he became convinced that the statements in the Gospels should be seen not as literal events but as mythological ideas. He expressed this concept in great detail in a work entitled *The Life of Jesus Critically Examined* (1835). His merciless criticism of the biblical texts were by no means meant to destroy the substance of the Christian faith, but rather to expose its authentic, unmythological truth by attributing the God-like qualities of Jesus not to Jesus alone but to the whole of humanity. Inevitably, Strauss was totally misunderstood, his work evoking a storm of protest. Apart from being seen as an attempt to undermine Christianity, the book was mistakenly interpreted as an instrument with which to promote Atheism. The unfortunate author was at once dismissed from his post, his academic career in ruins.

Today, a mere decade before the end of the twentieth century, blind faith in the literal word of the Gospel is on the wane. Scholars no longer jeopardise their entire careers should they openly question the Testament's historical accuracy, and among the educated, the ranks of the Fundamentalists are thinning.

In the mid-seventies, the leading investigator into the historicity of Christ was Professor George A. Wells who, in a volume published in 1975, asked *Did Jesus Exist?* With no outward hint regarding Hermetic knowledge, but apparently working logically from historical documents contemporary to the supposed period of Christ's ministry, Professor Wells concludes that the literal existence of the character Jesus is in doubt. He pleads with readers to set aside dogmatic beliefs and look into the question on their own account, the hope being that they will possibly arrive at a more enlightened outlook.

In support of the professor's findings I point out that if the Hermetic code is applied to some of his unanswered questions, further corroboration will present itself to confirm Jesus's fictional status. As a small but nevertheless significant example, Wells questions the use of the name Pontius Pilate. Jesus, he points out, was not linked with Pilate by writers contemporary to Pilate and his time in Judea, but only by those of seventy years later. Why? The reply to this – and one which will require the present reader to become familiar with the expositions laid out in the preceding volumes – is that those who concocted the Gospel fable seized upon the name because it was ideally opportune to do so. Pilate was indeed a real historical figure, a Roman procurator who governed in Judea during the ten years AD26 to 36. This coincided with the period selected by the Gospel writers for the character Jesus to conduct his ficticious ministry, and the inclusion of the name would lend some credibility to the story. But by far the most important reason was that the man's very name was too significant to ignore. In the scheme upon which the Hermetic code is founded, phonetic equivalents play a major part in conveying a hint of the secret principle. 'Pilate' was but a phonetic step away from the Latin 'pileus', a red cap worn by freed slaves. As the expositions have shown, the successful Hermeticist considered himself to be a 'freed slave' – freed that is, from the prejudice and false beliefs of his conscious mind which had previously imprisoned his understanding. Similarly, 'Pontius' easily equated with 'pontic', meaning 'bridging' (i.e. the bridging of the gulf between the conscious mind and the subconscious).

Other questions raised by Professor Wells, but left unanswered , could be resolved in the same way, although I concede that the explanation just offered will be far too tenuous for those yet to be acquainted with the intricacies of the allegorical code. In any event, it is now necessary to state that the ficticious character of the Gospels and the consequences of that revelation to the Fundamentalist is not the principal concern of this book. Of higher priority is the vexing question deliberately left without adequate explanation in *Hermes Unveiled* – what exactly is the 'transmission of consciousness'?

A broad hint was given in *The Language Of The Gods*, where the phrase 'transmission of consciousness' was replaced with 'development of the understanding'.

For those avid readers of books which purport to disclose

once and for all the ancient secrets of magic, sorcery, or the black arts, the phrase 'transmission of consciousness' doubtless conjured up visions of an entranced state in which the normal consciousness would be lifted to an exalted sphere, there to be endowed with a miracle-performing power or, at the very least, to converse with the angels. I hasten to state that the 'transmission' is not at all like that. At the very outset, when the decision to set down the text of *Hermes Unveiled* was made, the difficulties which stood in the way of successful communication to a readership were only too apparent. The entire field of occult literature was, and still is, contaminated with long-established, thoroughly misleading concepts, each new volume on 'magic' serving only to compound errors that are already monumental. So strongly entrenched have these fallacious ideas become that to assume them to be overthrown by the impact of a single book would have been unrealistic. It was decided, therefore, to split the work into three sections, it being wiser to commence at that level which is the current conception of the 'occult', and thereafter to proceed with a slow but steady erosion of false belief. Use of the phrase 'development of the understanding' was a step in the right direction, calculated to wean the reader away from any preconception of weird and wonderful mental transports supposedly associated with transcendental meditation. As with the first volume, the second made sure to warn against misunderstanding the original meaning of the nouns 'meditation' and 'contemplation', the modern interpretations of which are somewhat distorted from those of the past.

This third work, the completion of the trilogy, is designed to de-mystify much of the Hermetic scheme, the intention being to deliver to the reader a balanced and rational view of the principle to which the allegorical code refers. Alchemy is a natural 'magic' and it only requires an understanding free from preconception to master it. The 'Great Secret' is a secret no longer, having been adequately publicised since the turn of the century. The problem is that the majority simply do not recognise it for what it is.

Chapter One

It is accepted that the casual reader of Hermetic philosophy will have the greatest difficulty in crediting the work laid out in the two preceding volumes. In a wide range of expositions, unfamiliar concepts have been thrust to the fore, purely on the supposition that such a secret code exists. It was inferred that many well-known historical figures were secret Gnostics – St Paul, Richard III, Robert Boyle, Isaac Newton, Jonathan Swift, and even the writers Daniel Defoe, Victor Hugo, Mary Shelley and H. Rider Haggard. Further, it was stated that certain, well-established historical events were never real occurrences at all, but have been impressed as such on the public mind due to a gross misinterpretation of Hermetic allegory. Of these, easily the most controversial is the so-called life story of Jesus. It was asserted that lack of understanding of the true nature of the Gospel texts by the Council of Nicea in 325 A.D. subsequently delivered Catholics into centuries of theological ignorance.

Finally, and perhaps most mystifyingly, it was announced that the human mind, by application of the secret principle which the code proclaimed, could elevate itself at least one step higher in intuitive cognition. Mystifying though this latter concept is, I judge it to be the least unfamiliar, being merely an echo of statements made by a succession of noted philosophers down through the years. The monk Pernety, as an example, wrote as an alchemist when he made the following observation in *A Treatise On The Great Art*.

> Alchemy, properly speaking, is an operation of Nature, aided by Art. It places in our hands the Key to Natural Magic, or Physics, and renders us wonderful to men by elevating us above the masses.

Quite naturally, however, there was much scepticism. The great stumbling block was reached when the reader was asked to accept the fact of the code's existence, an act which required

belief in a principle not normally given the slightest credence.
Yet it is necessary to accept this principle before the code can
be completely understood.

Many have attested to the code's existence, even Hermetic
writers who are normally evasive on all other aspects of the
subject. Note, for instance, the anonymous author of *The
Sophic Hydrolith* (Water Stone of the Wise), an early
manuscript.

> But that the secret might not be lost, but rather continued
> and preserved, they expounded it most faithfully, both in
> their writings and in oral teaching to their faithful
> disciples, for the benefit of posterity. Nevertheless, they
> clothed and concealed the truth in allegorical language
> that even now only very few are able to understand their
> instruction and turn it to practical account.

For a second opinion, we may consult the *Theatrum Chemicum
Britannicum* of 1652, wherein Elias Ashmole writes of the
alchemists:

> Their chiefest study was to wrap up their *Secrets* in *Fables*,
> and spin out their *Fancies* in *Vailes* and *Shadows*, whose
> *Radii* seems to extend every way, yet so that they meet in
> a *Common Centre*, and point onely to one thing.

(sic)

To be sure, certain aspects of the code are not hard to
assimilate. Phonetic equivalents are just as common today, as
puns and companions of anagrams in the daily crossword
puzzle, as they were in the far past. But to accept without
question that the colours red, white and black are symbolic of
three aspects of a process which takes place wholly in the
human mind, is asking much of the reader. Nevertheless, the
use of the colour system is a fact vouchsafed for by no less a
person than the noted psychologist Carl Jung, who, in his
extensive researches into the mystery of Alchemy, indicated
that the stages of the mental process were originally four in
number, each one characterised by the original colours
mentioned in the writings of the Greek philosopher,
Heracleitus (500 BC) – *melanosis* (blackening), *leukosis*
(whitening), *xanthosis* (yellowing), and *iosis* (reddening).

This division of the process was called . . . the quartering of the philosophy. Later, about the 15th or 16th century, the colours were reduced to three, and the *xanthosis*, otherwise called the *citrinitas*, gradually fell into disuse or was but seldom mentioned. Instead, the *viriditas* sometimes appeared after the *melanosis* or *nigredo* in exceptional cases, though it was never generally recognised.

(Vol. 12, Collected Works, page 229)

Viriditas (green) is designated in the expositions as the colour of initiation, and as a prominent example of its use the reader may refer to the folk lore tale 'Gawain and the Green Knight'. In considering the reason for the presence of Hermetic symbolism, Jung concluded that:

A symbolism as rich as that of alchemy invariably owes its existence to some adequate cause, never to whim or play of fancy.

It is a carefully understated dictum with which all logical minds must concur, for its repeated application, the masterly inventiveness of the symbolism over such a vast period of time in so many areas of art, literature and architecture, points indisputably an underlying principle of high importance to those who have discovered it. In the far past, knowledge of this principle remained in the custody of men of wisdom, its revelation restricted to those who proved themselves mentally mature enough to receive it. And for many subsequent centuries the knowledge remained elusive, not necessarily by design of the initiates, but because – as the alchemists were fond of repeating – the Hermetic Secret guarded itself. Moreover, while world-wide communication of knowledge rested with the academics of each nation and their respective books, there was no reason to believe that the general mass of public would ever become fully aware of the Hermetic scheme. As time passsed, though, and improved education allowed a reading public slowly to develop, a point was reached where a full revelation of the Great Secret became imminent – not simply by way of a covert, allegorical reference that was understood by a few, but through a full and frank disclosure of the basic principle. A revelation of this magnitude did not emerge in one stroke of an author's pen. While allegories were still the Hermeticists' stock in trade, certain brief references, stated in an open manner, began to appear. More often than not, the authors, in fear of charges of heresy, even as late as the closing years of the 19th century, preferred to remain anonymous. But in America, where the shackles of Church doctrine were beginning to fall away, there was a bolder approach. William James, the noted psychologist and philosopher, a professor at Harvard University, produced a book in 1910 in which he stated in a single sentence the basic Hermetic principle, but it went unnoticed by most, the work itself appealing to a limited section of the reading public, and scarcely matching the popularity enjoyed by fiction writers of the time. Thus, at that particular period, the knowledge remained within a specific and exclusive circle.

In 1913, another notable attempt was made, this time by the English writer, Austin Osmand Spare. Born on New Year's Day 1889, the son of a London policeman, Spare was introduced to Hermetic theory at a very early age by a sensitive, a friend of the family. In his late teens, Spare began work on a full expression of the principle in a book which he entitled *The Book of Pleasure (Self-Love)*. With the subject still at that time steeped in mysticism and secrecy, he made use of sex and art in order to allegorise the Hermetic theme – hence the misleading title. Yet the mental principle was stated quite clearly, providing the reader was persevering enough to overcome the author's unorthodox style of grammar and syntax. Few, however, were offered the chance to unravel the truths within, for the work was privately printed and did not enjoy the circulation that might have been available from an established publisher. The beginnings of a real breakthrough occurred some nine years later.

In the early 1900s, while engaged in his occupation as a student of pharmacy, a most unusual experience befell the young Emile Coué. A patient suffering from an apparently intractable disease took a new patent medicine on Coué's advice – and was cured almost immediately. The young pharmacist was even more astonished when, after subjecting the medicine to analysis, he discovered it to be a harmless compound with no curative potential relative to the patient's ailment. Coué eventually realised that the cure was self-induced by the patient, a phenomenon brought about solely in response to the 'involuntary eloquence' with which he himself had prescribed the remedy. Without realising it at the time, he had implanted a hypnotic suggestion in the patient's mind.

The experience and the subsequent realisation of its import was to change the course of the pharmacist's career. In 1910 he set up a free healing clinic in the town of Nancy, there to practise and teach *autosuggestion*, his term denoting induced self-hypnosis. The success of the venture is a matter of historical record. Coué's catch-phrase 'every day, in every way, I'm getting better and better' is known the world over. In 1922, four years before his death, he explained the principles of his method in a paper entitled *Self Mastery Through Conscious Autosuggestion*, and it is this work which prepared the way for world wide revelation of the Hermetic secret. One of the key statements in Coué's text occurs in a passage comparing the conscious self to the subconscious self:

> . . . as it is the unconscious that is responsible for the functioning of all our organs by the intermediary of the brain, a result is produced which may seem paradoxical to you; that is, if it believes that a certain organ functions well or ill . . . the organ in question does indeed function well or ill. . . .

Further on Coué states that if autosuggestion is not working for a particular patient it is because the subject has not sufficient faith in the outcome, or is not saying the catch-phrase with the necessary conviction.

Here at last, then, in a book that would eventually be read by millions, was a bald, unequivocal statement of the means by which the legendary Philosophers' Stone could be attained – if it could be recognised as such. The whole thrust of Coué's work with autosuggestion was hinged upon the power of belief exerted by his patients upon themselves. Since the initial experience with the 'miracle' cure, a placebo, the ex-pharmacist had grasped this basic principle. This vital key was not understood immediately, for public attention was focussed more on the effects of autosuggestion, the miraculous or semi-miraculous cures that were achieved, rather than the cause. In the meantime the art of Hermetic allegory continued to confound and confuse, at the same time offering clues to the inner truth. One prominent example was penned by a French author who preferred to remain incognito, publishing instead under the name of Yram. As this is quite obviously 'Mary' in reverse, the author's hermetic background is duly acknowledged.

In the period between the first and second world wars, spiritualist circles on both sides of the Atlantic were actively engaged upon their respective investigations into the phenomenon of astral projection, or as it was latterly called, out-of-body experiences. A well publicised sequence was instituted by an American, Prescot F. Hall who, in 1908, commenced an examination of two friends who claimed to be able to project their astral bodies at will. Hall himself was a dabbler in spiritualism, and at the time was attending seances run by a non-professional sensitive, Mrs Minnie Keeler, who employed either automatic writing or the Ouija board to receive her 'communications'. Although she seemed disinterested in anything but the most superficial of psychic matters, she agreed to try and help. Thus, from the period 1908 until 1915, Hall received some 350 pages of automatic writing devoted to the subject of astral projection. These were duly published in an article written by Hall for the American Society for Psychical Research, Journal number ten, dated 1916.

Yram saw fit to capitalise on the current wave of interest for the subject, producing *Practical Astral Projection*, a work purporting to be from one who was able to project an astral double into higher worlds – and if read at face value by astral projection enthusiasts would yield no real information regarding the phenomenon other than that which was already known. But for those who well know the difference between the phenomenon and the specific mode of 'projection' on which Yram constantly discourses, the Hermetic principle is to be plainly discerned. Advising on how astral projections should be undertaken, the author writes:

. . . each one must discover the qualities which he must develop in order to master those conditions which are unfavourable to his existence. The first principle of the organisation, of this personal reform, is 'confidence'. . . .

To have confidence, as you hardly need reminding, is to have Belief. In the period from the middle of the 19th century up until the years immediately preceding the second world war, various circles of spiritualists, theosophists, psychologists and philosophers, both in Europe and America, employed a quaint phrase with which to express a certain form of meditation. It was called 'entering the Silence'. As a description of any metaphysical state is likely to beggar the imagination of the most literate, explanations of what the Silence was and how one could enter it were generally high in theological tone, but low in explicit direction. James Martineau, for example, the theologican and philosopher who held Unitarian pastorates in Liverpool and London, and who became principal of Manchester New College in 1869, advocated that the candidate should strip himself of all pretence, selfishness, sensuality and sluggishness of soul; lift off thought after thought, passion after passion, until he reached the innermost depths of all. Once there, in the Silence, it would be strange if the Eternal Presence was not felt close upon the soul. At this particular era, it must be stated, the inclination towards secrecy concerning the subject was still considerable, it being the wisest course in view of the power yet wielded by the Church. It was not until several decades later, after the general public's acceptance and interest in the work of Emile Coué, that the subject began to be discussed more openly – and far more explicitly. Of considerable assistance to the novice was a small volume which appeared in the late '30s, written by Helen Rhodes Wallace and entitled *How To Enter The Silence*. In full knowledge of the truth concerning the Hermetic process, the author correctly describes the entering of the Silence as

. . . the silencing of all unreality, of doubt, fear, false belief, worry, complaining, grief, of everything that is merely of the outer personality. . . .

The end result of this practice, readers are assured, would be an entering into relation with a creative process by which they might attain:

> . . . the knowledge and power to fill an idea with substance.

This state of mind is called Faith – no mere passive state of belief (by which the writer meant opinion), but a state of *Knowing*.

> Faith is not an intellectual belief in something, but a state of consciousness capable of transforming an invisible idea into living existence.

In retrospect, it would have been thought that Helen Rhodes Wallace's work, in all probability the first of its kind in that it was devoted solely to an explicit revelation of the Hermetic secret, would have been seized upon by a public eager to make use of the valuable information within. In fact, its circulation was restricted, for it was published by the Science of Thought Press, whose readership was largely confined to those who were interested or actively engaged in Spiritualism and its allied doctrines. Nevertheless, it may be judged a major step forward in the process of revelation, its influence undoubtedly preparing for the introduction of works which would prove to have more impact on the minds of the general reading public. The first of these made its appearance in 1948, when a New York publishing house produced *The Magic Of Believing* by Claude M. Bristol. With such a thought-provoking title, the book immediately attracted a readership from outside occult circles as well as from within. On the opening page, in a style that is as direct as it is lucid, a question is posed:

> . . . is there something – a force, a factor, a power, a science – call it what you will – which a few people understand and use to overcome their difficulties and achieve outstanding success?

The author then proceeds to describe in detail the magical power of Belief.

Even if the present reader has no knowledge of Claude Bristol, or his popular book, this whole theme must by now have invoked a feeling of familiarity. Quite obviously, we have arrived at a stage where *How To Enter The Silence* and *The Magic Of Believing* can be seen as precursors of an even more successful publication, *The Power Of Positive Thinking*, by Norman Vincent Peale.

Although well known today, Peale's work was not an instant best-seller if judged by modern standards, but after its first edition in 1953, more than two million copies were sold during the following twenty five years. It seemed that, at last, the Hermetic message was percolating through to the layman.

As a Christian minister from a quiet, mid-western town, Peale wrote from the parochial clergyman's point of view, rather than as someone who was Gnostically aware. The subconscious power was always referred to by the biblical terms 'God', 'the Lord', or 'The Presence', and the way to reach 'Him' was by the practise of constant 'prayer'. Doubtless the tenets expressed by Peale are well known to many, but for those who have never been inclined to read his book, it may be said that the Hermetic scheme – or, at least, one facet of it – was reduced to a three stage formula; Prayerise – Picturise – Actualise.

To 'prayerise' meant to establish a daily system of creative prayer directed at God. To 'picturise' entailed printing a picture of the desired object or state on the screen of your imagination and holding it there while 'surrendering to the will of God'. If the novice could carry out the first two stages successfully, that which was desired would sooner or later 'actualise' in the material environment. The all-important factor in the execution of the creative act was the realisation that faith is indispensable. Peale exhorts his readers, therefore, to 'practise believing'.

> Never use a negative thought in prayer. Only positive thoughts get results.

As with Claude Bristol, much of Peale's success with his book was due to its down to earth title, and indeed, the expression 'positive thinking' has assumed a prominent and lasting place in our language ever since.

As would be expected, similar manuals for the acquisition of success swiftly appeared, or had been introduced at about the same time. Dale Carnegie's *How To Win Friends And Influence People* became another well-established publication. What is seldom realised is the fact that the principle expounded within is none other than that of ancient Hermes, the same truth expressed by Emile Coué, but applied to successful living instead of healing.

In a singularly more academic tone, a method for success in life was offered by Dr Maxwell Maltz, a specialist in plastic surgery. In his 1960 publication, *Psycho-Cybernetics*, he related how he discovered that when he changed a person's features, it also incurred a change in the subject's 'self-image'. The self-image is what you believe yourself to be in your innermost thoughts – not what you might pretend to be when in the company of others.

> To really live, that is to find life reasonably satisfying, you must have an adequate and realistic self image that you can live with.

If the self-image is changed, the personality follows suit. The development of an adequate self-image, Dr Maltz maintains, will seem to imbue the individual with new capabilities and new talents which literally turn failure into success. This phenomenon caused him to take a more enlightened view of the principle of positive thinking. Less academic, blatantly more mercenary in approach, were such publications as *Think And Grow Rich*, by Napoleon Hill, or *Bring Out The Magic In Your Mind*, a 1964 volume written by professional magician, Al Koran. Despite its down-market aura in comparison to the approach of Dr Maltz, this latter work contains passages of the greatest interest to the Hermetic student, for it unexpectedly makes significant connections with the Old and New Testament. While discussing the techniques of mental visualisation, Koran suddenly refers his readers to a passage in Genesis.

> The oldest story of visualisation comes from the Bible – that of Jacob and the spotted cattle.

In due course this connection will be investigated, for it is of major importance.

The 1970s produced no further revelatory material from the

world of literature, although publications dealing with the subject were placed on the market from time to time. To mention but one we may quote *Macro-Mind Power*, a 1978 volume by Rebecca Clark which declared itself to give 'once secret techniques for releasing the macrocosmic power of your mind'. This work was no more than a reiteration of the central theme expounded by the previously mentioned works, the only difference being that good old-fashioned *Faith* (Belief/ Conviction) is referred to under the pseudo-scientific term 'Macro-Mind Power'. The fundamental issue which must now be contemplated is that the literary works so far examined are all manuals which, whatever terms may be used in whatever decade or century, are united in their purpose, the expression of the positive thinking principle.

It may require an even greater adjustment of mental attitude to accept that these works are merely late arrivals in a vast catalogue which has its origin at a time many thousands of years B.C. All historical manuscripts and documents that were the subject of exposition in *Hermes Unveiled* and *The Language Of The Gods* are, in reality, texts on the art of Positive Thinking – Greek myth, Old and New Testament, Alchemical tracts, the Rosicrucian Manifestoes, Nursery tales, Masonic ritual, and the rest. Religious fundamentalists, Christians who find it impossible to comprehend why their Gospel characters are declared ficticious, would begin to glimpse a very sound reason if, with minds freed from the cloying effects of theological indoctrination, they would admit that the crude death of a man in Jerusalem nearly two thousand years ago has no bearing on their present circumstances, nor does it offer them the 'salvation' so earnestly yearned for. But a Gospel story in which a novice can detect the tenets of positive thinking as applied to self, is a wonderful stepping stone to the goal of self-salvation, a guide to self-improvement of a magnitude far greater than has ever been offered by any Catholic pope.

Yet, as the alchemists truly stated, the Hermetic secret guards itself. The number of people who are able to give genuine credence to the concept of an active mind-power, to really believe in the power of belief, is still surprisingly small. While researching material for this work, I called in at my local public library to ask if they held a copy of *The Power Of Positive Thinking*.

'Ah, yes,' the assistant replied. 'I know we've got that book. When you've read that, you're supposed to be able to fly off the end of Brighton pier!'

Lightheartedly meant, as the remark undoubtedly was, it does typify the general attitude towards the concept of a mind influence which is not supported by visible, physical action. The fact that such a power is called into use every day by everyone is completely overlooked simply because, while the effect may be well noted, the cause is seldom recognised. And if the lay person entertains such scorn, how much more so the supposedly impartial academic? To equate positive thinking, perceived by many as a twentieth century fetish, with Greek philosophy, biblical Testaments, Gnosticism, Rosicrucianism, or the Grand Arcanum of Alchemy, is unthinkable. The truth of the matter is that the principle so openly expressed by Peale, Bristol, Rhodes Wallace and the others, is no modern psychological gimmick, but an essential facet of the human psyche that has functioned for as long as homo sapiens has existed. From this point of view, examination of the older texts will unarguably show that their sole purpose was to pass on knowledge of that particular principle which we recognise today as positive thinking. The common goal of both ancient and modern texts is to guide mankind towards a further, very important step in its slow evolution.

Chapter Two

It is the intention now to match modern texts on positive thinking with the old documents, thus showing that the purpose of both is identical; but before commencing, it is necessary to draw attention to the question of semantics in relation to the words 'faith' and 'belief'.

There are two opposing factors of the mind to which scant importance is ordinarily attached, but which are regarded as of the highest possible significance by the Hermetic initiate. These factors are Certainty and Doubt. Certainty is an attribute of the subconscious, while Doubt emanates from the reasoning capabilities of the conscious mind. As for the words 'faith' and 'belief', while they should be indicative of Certainty, in common speech there is always an element of ambiguity unless carefully defined at the time. As an example, someone may say of a new enterprise:

> 'One must have faith in the project. I believe it will be a success.'

From this you may infer that the speaker, whilst having high hopes, is not really certain of success – that there is an element of doubt in his mind, although he is of the opinion that the desired success will materialise. When the Hermetic initiate, on the other hand, employs the words Faith and Belief, he means an unqualified certainty which entertains not the slightest particle of doubt. In Hermetic parlance, he KNOWS. Having passed through the Hermetic process to become aware of his subconscious, he is acquainted with a knowing, positive certainty.

In the Hermetic thesis *Plotinus to Flaccus*, the 3rd century Greek philosopher, Plotinus, categorises the sensation of 'knowing' into three degrees – opinion; science; illumination:

> The means or instrument of the first is sense; of the second, dialectic; of the third, intuition. To the last I

subordinate reason. It is absolute knowledge founded on the identity of the mind knowing with the object known.

The sensation of 'knowing' is experienced by each one of us every day, but seldom if ever is its potential realised, nor is it subjected to analytical thought. As an instance, there is the crawling infant who sees other children and adults performing the seemingly impossible feat of balancing upright on two legs. In time, the infant emulates the feat and from that moment on, never gives another thought to the mechanics of walking because it KNOWS it can do it.

Particular Hermetic writers have taken the trouble to discuss this difficult point, in an effort to make their meaning clear. The 16th century initiate Paracelsus, who used the term 'divine wisdom' to define his subconscious power, fully recognised the ambiguity of 'faith' and 'belief'.

> If I know that divine wisdom can accomplish a certain thing, I might have the true faith, but if I merely believe that a thing might be possible, or if I attempt to persuade myself that I believe in its possibility, such a belief is no knowledge and confers no faith.

Just after the middle of the 19th century, Alphonse Louis Constant, better known to students of occult literature as Eliphas Levi, gave his own view:

> . . . we must separate our certitudes from our beliefs and distinguish sharply the respective domains of science and faith, realising that we do not know things which we believe, and that we cease immediately to believe anything which we come to know.

An alternative, perhaps less enigmatic approach, from Rosicrucian Franz Hartmann in the late 1800s, defines the Hermetic masters as 'knowers', specifying three distinct types. The first was the 'scientist' who dealt with opinions and illusory appearances. The second was those who were able to recognise interior truths by the power of their interior perception (understanding). The third category was the adepts

> . . . who are one with the truth and know everything

because they know themselves by the power of the Holy Ghost being manifest in themselves.

It is patently evident that these writers were attempting to portray a feeling of absolute conviction and certainty – a KNOWING – an emotional state where not only does Doubt have no place, but neither does hope, for hope implies uncertainty.

The word 'hope' also implies a future tense, a desire as yet unfulfilled – and this brings us to the most important and complex question of Time as related to the consciousness.

The 'God' of each and every religion, by whatever name it may be known, is always deemed to be immortal and eternal. In the Christian theological scheme, the Lord Almighty is often referred to as the Eternal Father, but it must be noted that the word 'eternal', as applied in the older texts, does not mean a state of time without end. Rather it is intended to indicate a state where there is no time to be measured in the normal manner – a state in which time cannot exist. The common distinction between 'mortal' (of the flesh) and 'immortal' (of the spirit) offers no real argument, but opponents of the concept of an eternal present insist that a state of time such as that in which the physical body lives, cannot exist side by side with a state of No-Time. As a reply, I can only point out that Time, as our consciousness perceives and measures it, always commences at that instant we call the 'present moment', or 'now', and then decays into the past. It is our personal 'I' which observes the present moment, our memory which recalls the past, and our imaginative faculties which allow us to anticipate the future; but of the three, the only true sense of *being* is our constant experiencing of the present moment. Appreciation of this phenomenon can be from two points of view. Either time is continually receding from the present moment (the observation point of the 'I'), in which case the latter is motionless in relation to moving time – or the personal 'I' (the present moment) is moving forward in time, leaving each second of material life to remain motionless as it is spawned. Whichever view is taken, one part is moving in time, whilst the other remains motionless (Timeless). Yet both states exist as an integral part of each other. Readers will, of course, argue this point for themselves, to draw their own conclusions, but for the purposes of this book, any philosophical statements made will be based on the assumption that it is the present moment which is Timeless.

It has long ago been declared that different men devote themselves to a study of Hermetic philosophy for different reasons. Many an alchemical treatise will inform its readers that the true philosopher is impelled by the love of Truth and an insatiable desire for wisdom, and that nothing more is sought. While this is manifestly true, it is more correct to assume that paramount in any novice's mind will be the desire to acquire knowledge of the method by which personal destiny can be influenced, thereby ensuring wealth and well-being. But is such control possible? Is thought power alone, without the aid of physical intervention, sufficient to alter the course of one's fate?

The philosophers of old were always ready to affirm the possibility, if not the means by which such control could be accomplished. In his work, *Mysteries of the Egyptians, Chaldeans and Assyrians*, the 4th century philosopher Iamblichus insisted that

> . . . the more divine part of man, which was formerly united to the gods by being aware of their existence, afterwards entered into the human state, becoming fettered with the bonds of necessity and fate. Hence it is requisite to consider how he may be released from these bonds. There is, therefore, no other dissolution of them than the knowledge of the gods.

The expression 'knowledge of the gods' is of the highest significance for the researcher, for translation into modern terms renders it 'the KNOWING of the subconscious'. Iamblichus also describes this as a 'special principle of the soul' which is superior to all nature and generation, and through which

> . . . we are capable of being united to the gods, of transcending the mundane order, and of participating in eternal life and the energy of the supercelestial gods. Through this principle, therefore, we are able to liberate ourselves from fate.

This is explicit as far as it goes, but perhaps a clearer idea of how beneficence might be attracted to the Hermetic philosopher was given in an anonymous preface to a 17th century collection of alchemical tracts called *The Hermetic Museum*. The writer declares that the initiate philosopher has the most effective means of becoming rich at his command, if only he cared to invoke it, but he is fired by the love of philosophy, caring nothing for 'the mocking grandeur of fortune'.

> So thought the Sages of Saracens, Egyptians, Arabs and Persians; for when they were oppressed by tyrants, and violently driven into exile, they protected and supported themselves by means of their Art, and through their knowledge of the transmutation of metals they had at their command not only sufficient to live upon, but all the comforts and pomp of life, and thus practically demonstrated that they could obtain all that gold and silver could give.

'Transmutation of metals' was a phrase used by alchemical writers to express the process of positive thinking, the exercise of the power of *knowing*.

Those who did master the method by which fate could be manipulated were not careless with the information. Such knowledge was regarded as the most precious gift of God, a holy Art, and kept from others as a matter of conscience. The traditional way by which the Gnosis was passed on to those who were worthy of receiving it was by means of the allegorical code alone. An extract from *The Sophic Hydrolith* gives the reason:

> For this practice they had a very good reason; they wished to force those who seek this wisdom to feel their dependence on God (in Whose hands are all things), to obtain it through instant prayer, and, when it had been revealed to them, to give all the glory to Him. Moreover, they did not wish the pearls to be cast before the swine. For they knew that if it were made known to the wicked world, men would greedily desire nothing but this one thing, neglect all labour, and give themselves up to a dissolute and degraded life.

To those unfamiliar with this knowledge, the idea of a magic power which can grant wishes seems to stem directly from the pages of Arabian Nights. Yet it has been declared a reality in both ancient and modern texts which are far removed from fiction or fantasy. Peale, in his *The Power of Positive Thinking*, explains that the process is simply a matter of imagining the desired circumstances in your mind, assuming a belief in them (i.e. convincing yourself that the desired scenario is 'actualising' itself), and waiting until they become a reality in your material world – and while this analysis is unquestionably correct, it is apparent that an accomplishment of such a desirable process is not as easy as it is made to seem, otherwise all who had read Peale's book would now be millionaires and advising others on how to duplicate the feat.

The hard fact of the matter is that no one can give precise instructions for success because the process is one that is instituted by, and takes place in, the individual's own area of inner thinking. Thus, the onus is on the individual alone to develop his or her understanding, rather than to expect revelation to come from a book or a teacher. The alchemists of the Middle Ages referred to this development of the understanding as the 'making of a vase', repeatedly admonishing the candidate to 'make his vase himself', the double meaning of which must now be apparent to the present reader. When finished, this *vase* would contain the *waters* of Truth and Wisdom (Gnosis).

A principal requisite for success is for the novice to rid his mind of prejudice and false opinion – to open the way for the mind to believe in Belief. Only when this has been accomplished can a move forward into actual practice be made with any reasonable expectation of success. Emile Coué, when expounding his practical application of the process as a healing technique, was careful to underline the fact that autosuggestion would not work for those unwilling to understand the importance of confidence (Belief).

The initial step towards success in the Hermetic venture, as recommended by Eliphas Levi, is 'isolation' – by which he meant mental isolation, a distancing of oneself. He advocated complete independence of opinion; never to be influenced by the ideas of others; never to subjugate yourself to any human cause; to have no emotional ties; and to develop a perfect self-restraint of the senses.

This sounds a little more daunting in prospect than the easy-going advice of Al Koran, who advises readers merely to

> Cultivate a strong belief, be absolutely positive and you will release this wonderful magic power. . . .

Eliphas Levi's seemingly extreme outline is in acknowledgment of the fundamental Force which animates all sentient life, the force we call 'God', with its ever-present influence over all. It is a principle that must be touched on before proceeding.

From time immemorial, the sages have urged mankind to 'Know' oneself. To quote a single example from historical sources, the 3rd century Church Father, Hippolytus, cites Arabian philosopher Monimus as saying

> Abandon the search for God and the creation and other matters of a similar sort. Look for him by taking yourself as the starting point. Learn who it is who within you makes everything his own and says 'My God, my mind, my thought, my soul, my body'. Learn the sources of sorrow, joy, love, hate. Learn how it happens that one watches without willing, rests without willing, becomes angry without willing, loves without willing. If you carefully investigate these matters you will find him in yourself.
>
> (*Refutation of All Heresies*, VIII 15, 1–2)

The reason for this injunction to soul search has nothing to do with everyday good, or bad, morality, but was given in the hope that self-analysis might reveal to the novice the presence of a factor seldom considered in the normal course of daily existence. It is that our movements and emotions are governed from within by means of a series of impulses that we continually receive and act upon. Our physical bodies, as we go through life, are like puppets on strings, and we have no idea who – or rather *what* – is pulling the strings.

The common ignorance of this fact was emphasized by Hermetic initiates of a particular period when, within their allegorical structure, they made use of the term 'ludibrium'.

The general idea of physical Man as merely an actor in a

passing 'drama' stemmed from Asiatic philosophy in which the candidate for illumination was advised never to identify with the 'drama' or become bond slaves to its materialistic allurements, for the belief that the physical world around us is the ultimate reality is misplaced. In truth it is no more than a grand illusion. The same concept was enlarged upon by a young writer of early 17th century Bohemia who saw mankind as no more than 'playactors'. A mere two years after the appearance of the *Fama*, and the *Confessio*, the famed Rosicrucian Manifestos which excited all Europe in 1614 and 1615, a third manuscript was published, a strange alchemical romance entitled *The Chemical Wedding of Christian Rosencreutz*. Author Johann Valentin Andreae, himself described it as a *ludibrium*, a fiction, a jest of little worth. More interestingly, in other texts, Andreae frequently applied the same term to the whole of the Rosicrucian movement, using phrases like 'the ludibrium of the Fama', or 'the ludibrium of the Confessio'. Subsequent commentators on the Rosicrucian Furore have taken Andreae's remarks at face value, concluding that the Manifestos were no more than an elaborate but pointless hoax. Others, however, have taken the trouble to look closely at the whole range of Andreae's literary endeavour, discovering a marked inconsistency regarding his opinion of entertainers in general. Certainly, when writing of the Rosicrucian Brotherhood, he seemed to be denigrating them by referring to them as 'mere players, comedians, frivolous and foolish people', derisive terms which apparently reflected a low opinion of all theatricals. Yet, in other writings, he highly praises players, plays and dramatic art, declaring them to be socially and morally valuable.

To resolve this inconstancy we have only to recall the fact that Johann Valentin Andreae's name was on the list of Grand Masters of that ancient and most secret of Rosicrucian lodges, the Priory of Sion. Thus, any remarks made by him in respect of the Rosicrucian Brotherhood will undoubtedly be in an allegorical context. And so it is with *ludibrium*. It is a Latin word from which the English 'ludicrous' is derived, and simply means a 'play', a 'joke', or 'a sense of foolishness'. However, used as it is in this instance by a Hermetic master, it will have two other meanings for those who are able to recognise them. The first is in direct relation to the Rosicrucian Manifestos, including Andreae's own *Chemical Wedding*, and it is a warning that the texts conceal a 'play' on words – i.e. the allegorical code in which all three manuscripts are written. The second refers to the facet of Hermetic philosophy which regards physical man as a mere actor whose movements on the stage of life are directed by something other than the conscious self.

Many others have dropped the same disguised hint, including even Guy de Maupassant, who concluded his *Private Affairs of Bel Ami*, with the words

We are all puppets unless we believe.

It is a common mistake to imagine that we consciously decide upon each act taken in daily life, but if sufficient pause for reflection is allowed, it will be realised that the directions come from inner impulses. If we believe that we are acting on our own account, it is because our conscious self is in accord with the impulse being obeyed at the time. It is not unknown, however, for us to obey an impulse which is entirely contrary to our will of the moment. An excellent if somewhat dramatic example of this, and one which can be verified if it is so wished, is a sequence of events that occurred in Michigan, USA, during September 1979. Jim Olesak, an engineer, was on his way from Chicago to visit his elderly mother, a four hundred mile journey by road. With ninety miles still to drive, he suddenly and inexplicably turned off the main highway with the intention of visiting his 70 year old cousin, Steve Hoholik. Just why he undertook the long and difficult detour, he could not say, for the two men were not close and had not seen each other for many years. Eventually he found his way to the Hoholik farm, arriving to find the farmhouse door swinging open, the place deserted. Obviously, Steve was out working somewhere on the 200 acre farm land. Feeling slightly foolish, Olesak returned to his car, intending to resume his journey. But something made him pause and then begin walking out into the fields. After about a mile, he reached the top of a small hill where, just over the brow, he saw a tractor. His cousin was lying with his right leg trapped beneath one of the machine's huge rear tyres. He had been there for twenty five hours after the tractor had rolled backwards as he was loading it with firewood. Doctors at the Manistique hospital confirmed that if it had been left there for much longer, his leg would have required amputation. Steve Hoholik told how he had shouted for help in vain, only too well aware that his nearest neighbours were miles distant.

'I was sure I was going to die out there, and I prayed. Then I saw Jim. It was strange. I hadn't seen him for thirty years and I didn't even recognise him at first.'

Jim Olesak could not explain what caused him to make a completely unintentional visit to his cousin's farm, the only rational answer to him being that it was just a lucky coincidence.

It is plain that he received an impulse which, despite the preplanned intentions of his conscious mind, he felt bound to obey. What remains to be determined is the means by which the impulse was initiated and how it was transmitted to him.

The Hermetic point of view does not recognise 'coincidence', maintaining that each and every action by all animate life is part of a meaningful pattern of events. The extent of this pattern and the mechanics by which it operates will become more clear as we proceed, but at this stage it may be comprehended as part of the philosophy expounded so many centuries ago by the Egyptian initiate priests and bequeathed to posterity in the allegorical tale of Isis and Osiris as I have outlined it in *Hermes Unveiled*. To state this philosophy in modern terms, we might envisage every human mind as a transmitter and receiver of electro-magnetic impulses, operating on a waveband which is ostensibly not discernable by the physical sense. I use the word 'ostensibly' because such impulses *can* be detected by the conscious mind, but not until it has been trained to do so. Assuming that such a waveband exists, and the Hermetic initiates assure everyone that it does, then it is but a step to the recognition that the individual subconscious minds of all are interconnected, with the attendant possibility of one individual receiving a transmission from another. The conscious minds of both sender and receiver may not be aware of the communication taking place, except perhaps as a vague feeling of 'knowing' that something is happening without being able to state exactly what it is.

Understandably, it is hard to place credibility in the concept of a waveband of invisible energy, especially as it is undetectable by that established criterion of proof, the scientific instrument. In his work, *The Book of Pleasure*, Spare attempted to give some guide to recognition of the waveband's basis:

> You are conscious of the gay Butterfly you observe, and you are conscious of being 'You'; the Butterfly is conscious of being 'itself' and as such is a consciousness as good as and the same as yours, i.e. of your being 'you'. Ergo – you are one and the same – the mystery of mysteries and the most simple thing in the world to understand.

Having passed through the required stages of self-analysis, the Hermetic initiate learns to enlarge upon this concept, recognising the reception of an impulse as the feeling we call 'intuition'. The means by which we may consciously transmit an impulse, on the other hand, is by the exercise of positive thinking, the feeling of 'knowing' deliberately manufactured within the mind. Thus, if you remain constantly on the alert for the slightest feeling of intuition, and if you are capable of manufacturing the feeling of 'knowing' in sufficient intensity, then you will be in mental contact with the invisible waveband, the collective subconscious.

Admittedly this principle is easy to state on paper. For those who have the wisdom to overrule natural prejudices and to retain an open mind, the principle is not hard to grasp. But actually to put it into practice, to activate the dormant power of the mind by learning how to control the invisible energy of thought and feeling, and to put it to work on your own behalf, is far from simple because it demands a complete readjustment of mental outlook – an *upheaval*, just as the allegories have so often indicated. You are required to believe implicitly in that which has hitherto been unbelievable. Each person bears within them the potential to create given circumstances in the material world, just as God is said to create, and it is for this reason that the alchemists exhorted others to 'know' themselves, for that power which everyone calls 'God' is to be found only in one's own mind, resident there for as long as physical life lasts. In the 18th century, the Comte de St Germain was considered to have blasphemed when he declared

> . . . in the same way that God created the world, so too I can conjure forth everything I wish from the void.

In those days, superstitious fear of the unknown and abysmal ignorance of the true nature of mankind ensured that the Count was accused of sorcery. Today, we would recognise him as a master in the art of positive thinking.

The Hermetic process, simply stated, is this: if you require something in this material world, and it can be reasonably available to you, all you have to do is to transmit that desire to your subconscious mind and its great and unlimited power will provide it for you. But the subconscious mind can only act in this astonishing manner if your desire is successfully transmitted to it from the conscious mind. In this operation the great stumbling block, the paradox that you are required to deal with, is that to cause the desire to reach the subconscious, the conscious mind must cease to exercise the desire, for as long as the conscious mind *wants* something, the very act of wanting implies a future tense in regard to fulfillment. The subconscious only deals with the eternal present moment, and therefore any idea which is offered in a non-present moment context will be rejected by it. Thus, the desire, in order to allow successful implantation in the subconscious, must be thought of as *already satisfied*. Only by believing that it has already been granted can your wish come true. By cultivating the factor of Certainty within your mind, you will gain inlet to the subconscious, but any trace of Doubt will render your desire impotent.

This difficult tenet of positive thinking is presented in the plainest possible terms, in Mark 11, verse 24:

> Therefore, I say unto you, What things soever ye desire, when ye pray, believe that ye receive them, and ye shall have them.

It is also possible, if sufficient study is devoted to the project, to discover the same open message within the most enigmatic of alchemical texts, although, as one would expect, phrased in a slightly more obscure manner. Take as an example, *The Golden Tract*, an anonymous manuscript of 1625. Following a series of quotations from established and suitably mystifying Hermetic texts, the author concludes the first section of his work with the words

> . . . if you know the beginning, the end will duly follow by the help of God. . . .

In order to interpret this correctly, the word 'know' must be construed as the act of 'knowing' (i.e. positive thinking), and not in its usual sense. Also substitute the words 'subconscious power' in place of 'God'.

A second extract from the same work advises readers to

> Cease to think of many things. Nature is satisfied with one thing, and he who does not know it is lost.

The exhortation to think of 'one thing' means to be of one mind – that is, to eradicate doubt and exercise positive thinking. And once again the hidden meaning of the word 'know' must be employed. A passage of similar interest may be found in a 'chemical treatise' of 1477, entitled *Ordinal of Alchemy*. Its author, Thomas Norton, saw fit to sub-title the work *Believe – Me*, an addition which no doubt baffled those unacquainted with the Hermetic principle of Belief with its eternal 'I'. Several helpful passages are to be discovered in this volume, such as:

> The first cause of sorrow (among the adepts) is to see and realise that among the many who seek this Art only few ever find it, and that no one can attain this knowledge unless he be taught before he begins.

The paradox within the last sentence is meant to project the reader's attention to the paradoxical nature of the Hermetic process, where one is required to believe that a desired situation exists before it can be made to materialise in the physical world.

In chapter three of the same work, Norton moves a little further towards complete revelation – provided the reader has the perspicacity to appreciate the subtlety:

. . . few will believe that it is a pearl of great price, for it is known to none but the wise. Thus I have laid bare to you a great secret, more plainly than any of the dead masters.

In his book *The Great Secret*, Eliphas Levi made a similarly covert contribution, first by preparing the way with a sentence which read

Learn to will what God wishes, and everything you want will certainly happen.

And then, a few paragraphs later, adding

So if you wish to reap on the left hand, sow on the right hand, and meditate on this piece of advice, which looks like a paradox and will give you a hint of one of the greatest secrets of occult philosophy. If you desire to attract, make a vacuum.

Readers may feel that this is just a little too obscure to be counted as the same principle expressed in Mark 11, 24, and it is true that the text of *The Great Secret* hardly deviated from the course dictated by Hermetic allegory. In *The Doctrine Of Transcendental Magic*, however, the same author could not have written more frankly:

In order to accomplish a thing we must believe in our possibility of doing it. . . . The operator, in a word, must realize in his whole life that which he wishes to realize in the world without him; he must become a MAGNET to attract the desired thing; and when he shall become sufficiently magnetic, let him be assured that the thing will come of itself, and without thinking of it.

The heavily accented use of the word 'magnet' in the passage leads us to an understanding of one of alchemy's prime symbols, *Magnesia*. To become an Alchemist, the candidate must generate within himself a 'magnesia', which is Hermetic parlance for a magnetic power to attract and 'coagulate' the invisible impulses of the collective subconscious. The proven initiate will confirm that this power is only possessed by those who are 'reborn in spirit' (have generated the power of Faith/Belief within their own minds).

Another helpful sentence can be found within the manuscript known as *The Testimony Of Helvetius*, a 17th century Hermetic fable. In fact, 'Helvetius' was a pseudonym adopted by a medical practitioner named Johann Friedrich Schweitzer, at one time physician to the Prince of Orange. The *Testimony* is a fiction, it being Hermetic allegory from start to finish. Its central character is a *stranger* (the subconscious) who claimed to be able to *make gold* (accomplish the process). But sandwiched in between the lines of allegory is a clue to the reality of the mental process, given when the stranger is made to say

> . . . for unless thou knowest the thing from the head to the heel, from the eggs to the apples; that, from the very beginning to the very end, thou knowest nothing; and though I have told thee enough, yet thou knowest not how the philosophers do make and break open the glassy seal of Hermes. . . .

Plainly, this is a re-statement of the theme, 'you must *know* before you can begin' (you must learn to apply the power of Certainty before you can succeed in the Hermetic process). In carefully placing such guidelines within a work of fiction, the author was following a routine already long established by early Hermeticists, the truth of this being discernable in the New Testament story of Jesus healing a boy who suffered with convulsions (Mark 9, 17–29). The boy's father asked for help from Jesus and the reply was given, in verse 23:

> Jesus said unto him, If thou canst believe, all things are possible to him that believeth.

The Hermetic significance of this statement – that is, its relevance to positive thinking – is lost if read only in the context of the story, as is the sentence in Schweitzer's *Testimony*. But both messages, taken on their own as they are meant to be, are identical and perfectly clear in intent.

The text of Peale's *The Power Of Positive Thinking* will advise readers to picture their desired goal in mind, to believe in its possibility, and to work towards its accomplishment with enthusiasm. It is the noun 'enthusiasm' which uncovers a further aspect of the initiate's symbolism. I need hardly stress that, to have enthusiasm for a project is to believe in it with some fervour, and therefore an undeniable relationship between 'enthusiasm' and 'faith' exists. The archaic meaning of 'enthusiasm' offers a helpful line of research for the student of Alchemy. The word is derived from the Latin 'enthusiasmus' and from the Greek 'enthousiasmous', 'enthousiazein' and 'entheos', meaning a god-inspired zeal, to be inspired, or possessed by God. On rare occasions the word was utilised by Hermetic writers as a means to convey the Science, as in an example set by the German philosopher, Heinrich Khunrath, in his *Confessio* (1596). In the first section of the tract, the author summarises his search for the True Stone of the Philosophers, describing how he had worked to solve the problem of Alchemy for twenty three years, during which time he had worked diligently in his laboratory, burning many a fine load of coals. He had been forced to put his hands in lime and coal, to build stoves and tear them down again, and to have broken many large and small glasses and retorts for distilling. He had travelled far in search of experts who might teach him, spending much before receiving finally

. . . the gift of Distinction in this Art of God. . . .

All this, as you may perceive, is an exercise in the allegorical language of the initiate. But in the next paragraph, Khunrath writes:

If any say I am merely an enthusiast because of this book of visions and extraordinary spiritual revelations, you are only a foolish dreamer who does not know or consider what the word 'enthusiast' really means. It is the Divine Breath. . . .

By 'Divine Breath', the author refers to Inspiration, making a play of both its meanings. Quite clearly Khunrath is telling his readers that his search for the Philosophers' Stone was successfully concluded after a study of enthusiasm (faith/ belief/positive thinking) and its effects. Corroboration of this conclusion is given later in the text, when the author states

To those who understand, the matter is easy. It can be taught and learned in one day – in fact, in one hour. All that is necessary to be known could be put in six or twelve lines. Bernhard says: 'I tell you that, whose eyes God opens to understand the Science, would be ashamed at the roundabout ways which are used, for it is so easy, one would scarcely believe it a play for children, a work for women'. . . .

Quite obviously this 'play for children, work for women' is not a reference to long years spent working in a chemical laboratory. Inspiration, the Divine Breath, is a factor of the mind, not of the work bench.

Before proceeding, it is best to qualify Khunrath's assertion that the Hermetic work can be taught in a short time. What he really means is that the principle can be expounded in two or three sentences. Carrying it out in practice, though, is a different matter. The analogy of physical breath/Divine Breath is ludicrously simple, once it has been explained. To 'inspire' means to breath in, or to draw air into the lungs, and human breath can be regulated so that it can be either hot or cold when expelled. Similarly, spiritual 'inspiration', or enthusiasm, can be hot or cold (totally dedicated, or half-hearted). Only 'hot' enthusiasm will have the desired effect, and that is why such enthusiasm is otherwise called the Secret Fire of the Philosophers. An alternative word for enthusiasm is 'zeal', a piece of obvious information, but which may help the alert reader to understand why Josephus called his Assassins *zealots*.

A companion word, with more than one meaning, seized upon by the Alchemists to be used in relation to their Divine Breath symbolism, is 'aspiration'. The great Rosicrucian, Paracelsus, referred to it in its Hermetic context when he advised that real and effective prayer is not lip prayer, but exaltation of thought and aspiration – and this may give a clue to the reason why Steve Hoholik's prayer was successful, uttered as he lay trapped beneath the wheel of his tractor. Despite statements later made to the Press ('I was sure I was going to die out there'), he obviously did not think so negatively at the time. When he prayed, he did not merely hope that 'God' would rescue him, he *believed* so, and thus his desire was successfully – if involuntarily – transmitted from the conscious mind to that all-powerful Force, the collective subconscious. The art of the alchemist is to accomplish the same transmission, but with conscious knowledge of the transaction. As Paracelsus has written:

> Alchemy is the art of becoming conscious of God with yourself.

To re-phrase that in the language of today, the subject is required to realise within the mind an acceptance of the potential power of positive thinking. By doing so, contact with 'God', the subconscious Force, can eventually be made. Unfortunately, it is a fact of life that our reasoning faculties (the conscious mind), active since birth and ever more so as each year of physical existence passes, is the one thing that will stand in the way of successful communication with the Force.

There are two factors which constitute unassailable barriers to contact with the subconscious. The first of these is Doubt, the presence of which is always part of the reasoning process, and it is for this fact alone that the Hermetic writers urged their readers to 'abandon reason'. The second is the element of Time, in particular the way we think of it.

Treating them in that order, we may agree that to be certain of something is to be of *one mind*, whereas to entertain doubt is to be of a divided mind. Even Opinion has a foundation of doubt, as the adept writers have always been ready to point out. Paracelsus was explicit, while Heracleitus merely declared Opinion to be

> . . . a falling sickness of the mind.

In the previous two volumes I have laid bare the extensive scope of Hermetic symbolism, reducing all to its common foundation, the Dualist philosophy, Good versus Evil. At this point I can now further qualify that by adding that Certainty is the foundation stone of Good, while Doubt acts in a similar respect for Evil. The importance of this dual aspect of the mind is forever underestimated, in spite of repeated efforts by philosophical scribes to draw attention to it. In his volume, *The Perennial Philosophy*, Aldous Huxley makes a pertinent comment:

. . . how significant it is that in the Indo-European languages . . . the root meaning of 'two' should connote badness. The Greek prefix 'dys' (as in dyspepsia) and the Latin 'dis' (as in dishonourable) are both derived from 'duo'. The cognate 'bis' gives a pejorative sense to such modern French words as *bevue* ('blunder', literally 'two-sight'). Traces of that 'second which leads you astray' can be found in 'dubious', 'doubt', and *Zweifel* – for to doubt is to be double-minded.

The New Testament, in its role as a treatise on positive thinking, naturally abounds with references to the evil nature of Doubt. Only difficulties in translation have rendered them obscure to modern eyes. As an example, we may consult the text of Matthew, chapter six, where Christ is preaching his sermon on the mount.

22. The light of the body is in the eye; if therefore thine eye be single, thy whole body shall be full of light.
23. But if thine eye be evil, thy whole body shall be full of darkness. If therefore the light that is in thee be darkness, how great is this darkness.

The original meaning of the symbolic 'eye' in this passage is 'conscious mind', while 'light' is obviously 'power of the subconscious'. Verse 22 tells us that if we remain of one mind ('Certainty') we will be able to make use of our subconscious power. The next verse warns that if the conscious mind is 'evil' (entertains Doubt), we will be cut off from the *'light'* (understanding) of the subconscious. And having stated this, it may now become more clear why Jesus is made to say 'get thee behind me, Satan'.

Interestingly enough, this quote from Matt. 16, 23, is followed by the words:

. . . thou are an offence unto me. . . .

In the Revised Version of the Gospel texts, this particular use of the word 'offence' has been coupled with its alternative 'stumbling-block', which itself is translated thus from the Greek 'scandalon', the word from which our present day 'scandal' is derived. It is nowadays generally agreed among biblical scholars that 'scandalized', as used in the Testament texts, means 'prevented from believing'. It was a conclusion reached only reluctantly, for it puzzled many scholars.

In both the previous volumes, I have endeavoured to make it quite clear that the Gospel text is a fable, and that the twelve Disciples never existed as real entities, but are characters invented by the Hermetic authors in order to portray collectively the reasoning and thinking aspect of the conscious mind. Peter is one such, and when Jesus (characterising Good – the subconscious) is made to say: 'Get thee behind me, Satan', it is a device to demonstrate the difference between the subconscious and the conscious in relation to the scheme of positive thinking. It is made even more clear by the addition of the sentence; 'Thou art an offence unto me' (you are a *stumbling-block* to me). Jesus (Good/Certainty) rejects Peter (Satan/Evil – the conscious mind) because he *prevents believing*.

An even more explicit example can be found in John 20, verse 29, concerning the disciple Thomas. The meaning of the name Thomas is 'twin', and it has long been assumed that this referred to the disciple being the twin brother of Jesus, but the true intent by the selection of the name was to indicate the dual aspect of the conscious mind – of which Thomas, like Peter, is representative. Thomas, or Doubting Thomas, as he is often named, characterises Doubt in the Gospel scheme of symbolism. And Jesus clearly states the tenets of positive thinking when he is made to say:

> 29. . . . Thomas, because thou hast seen me, thou hast believed; blessed are they that have not seen and yet have believed.

As I have previously indicated, the words 'blessed' and 'annointed' in the biblical texts refer to those initiates who have achieved the Hermetic process (have understood and made use of the power of positive thinking). You will note that, in the above verse, Thomas is not *blessed*, for he always doubts and must see before he will believe. But others who visualise their desires in their imagination and believe that they will materialise in their physical environment, are *blessed*. To sum it up, Jesus characterises Certainty, while Thomas characterises Doubt.

The second important factor which constitutes a great

barrier to successful positive thinking, is the element of Time as related to our thought processes. The Alchemists wrote sparingly of this, for it is the most secret of Hermetic lore. Briefly summarised at this point, it will be introduced later at the appropriate juncture. Owing to the faculty of memory, we can think in the past tense, while imagination allows us to venture into a possible future. Both, however, invite failure in the art of positive thinking. Emile Coué insisted that, if there were alternative wording of his formula, there must be no negatives and no future tense. If you wish for a desired state, or hope that it will come to pass, you are automatically thinking in the future tense. As long as you *want* something, and the want remains unfulfilled, your aspirations are centred on the future and cannot be transmitted to the *eternal now* of the subconscious. Austin O. Spare, in *The Book Of Pleasure*, puts it succinctly:

. . . Desire nothing and there is nothing you shall not realise. . . .

Chapter Three

The mere mention of positive thinking, the magical power of faith, is likely to draw a raised eyebrow or two, if not provoke outright scepticism. Yet, on all sides, both in our time and in those of past eras, are to be found instances of the power at work. The most common manifestation, and one to which the least significance seems to be attached, is the placebo. Emile Coué, in light of his experience of a miraculous cure effected by an ineffective compound, moved on to the concept that all medicines are, to a certain extent, worthless without the power of the patient's own belief to assist them. The medical profession may refute this, but take as an instance a cure recorded by Californian hypnotherapist, Melvin Powers. In a discussion about medical practice and the influence of hypnotism, a nurse told Powers of a patient who attended a clinic for electric diathermy treatment to cure an ailing shoulder. The patient was directed to the couch and the diathermy unit applied, after which the nurse left him to attend to other duties. Later she returned to switch the machine off, asking the patient how he felt. The man assured her that he felt a great deal better for the treatment. Later, after the patient had departed, and when the nurse was making a last check on the equipment before leaving herself, she was greatly amused to notice that the mains power supply plug of the diathermy unit was not in its socket. She recalled disconnecting it early that morning and remembered clearly that she had not re-inserted it for the patient's treatment. Yet the man had been convinced that the machine had been turned on and that the treatment had helped to ease his pain.

In this particular instance no medication was involved but the power of Belief still supplied the same 'miracle' cure.

The field of hypnotherapy is, of course, closely allied to the concept of positive thinking and therefore it comes as no surprise to find that the texts of Powers' books contain a number of pointed references to the need for belief.

Hypnosis will not work with skeptics (unbelievers)

Above all, the hypnotist must have complete *confidence* in himself.

You must *believe* that you can conquer your difficulties no matter how long you have had them.

Some subjects for hypnosis do not succumb unless the hypnotist employs techniques of an exaggerated kind as shown on films. The subjects *believe* that this is the only way in which they can be hypnotised.

Initiates of bygone eras have made great use of the placebo experience as a method of passing on knowledge about the power of belief. Sir Francis Bacon, a highly advanced adept of positive thinking, left the following quaint anecdote. Since early childhood, he said, there had been a wart on his hand, but at the age of sixteen, while living in Paris, the solitary wart suddenly became accompanied by a cluster of others, so that within a month, more than a hundred had appeared. The wife of the English Ambassador, upon learning of the young Bacon's misfortune, offered to help him disperse them. She obtained a piece of lard, rubbed the warts with it and then nailed it to her window, facing south and in the rays of the sun. The lard, of course, gradually melted and disappeared. At the same time, within five weeks, all Bacon's warts had disappeared, including the ancient, solitary one.

The veracity of this story cannot be proven, but it is in the novice's interest to accept it for what it is, an example of involuntary activation of the subconscious power through positive thinking. The young Bacon was so impressed by the unusual ritual undertaken on his behalf that he inwardly *believed* in its power to cure. In fact, his subconscious mind, after successful impregnation, effected the cure because it has control over all bodily functions.

The chemist Robert Boyle, a Rosicrucian and also holder of the position of Grand Master to the Priory of Sion Lodge, related an experience of his own which, he maintained, changed his whole mode of thought.

At nine years of age he was suffering a period of delicate health, enduring recurring bouts of sickness. On one occasion, when he was recovering from a bout of fever, his doctor prescribed a tonic, but by an error, the dispenser made up a violent emetic. The effects of a large dose in his already weakened state was so drastic that the physician feared for the child's life. Although Boyle recovered, the incident laid within him a deep distrust of all doctors and medicines. At the age of eleven, he was again taken ill, to recover only after a long period of poor health. Almost on the point of recovery, he was terrified to learn that his doctor had prescribed a laxative. Vivid memories of his previous experience served to convince him that the medicine would only make him worse – a point of view well known to the young serving maid whose duty it was to attend him. Out of compassion and saying nothing to the boy, she emptied the draught away, substituting his favourite drink, prune juice. But so thoroughly convinced was Robert that he even found the prune juice revolting. The maid was so amused at this that she told the boy what she had done. Boyle, too, was highly amused, but also deeply impressed at the way his sense of taste and smell had been deceived by prejudice. The incident fostered a lasting distrust of practical medicine and throughout his life, he devoted considerable time to the invention of cures which would render the services of a doctor unnecessary. Some five hundred 'prescriptions' were left to posterity, most of which appear to be founded on the art of witchcraft rather than medicine. For an example, as a cure for jaundice, he recommended the hanging up of a sheep's gall bladder into which two or three drops of the patient's urine had been introduced. As the bladder dried up, so would the jaundice leave the patient. It is easy to recognise the same principle at work here as with Francis Bacon's warts. Materially, the use of a sheep's gall bladder is meaningless. It is the ritual which is intended to bluff the patient into believing a cure by this means is possible. If the belief can be transmitted to the patient's subconscious, then a cure will be brought about.

The reader may protest that these 'cures' are no better than witchcraft or black magic, and the protest is justified. What else is witchcraft or black magic but the activation of the subconscious power through Belief? The subconscious does not recognise human moral values of good or bad in its response. It merely carries out the directives which are transmitted to it. This may explain why, when Robert Boyle wrote to Sir Isaac Newton to discuss the advisability of publicly making clear the secret information, Newton was less than enthusiastic:

> . . . because the way in which mercury may be so impregnated, has been thought fit to be concealed by others that have known it. . . .

Newton's 'mercury' is that of the old alchemists, the subconscious power which may be 'impregnated' by an idea or desire from the conscious mind – if the conditions are right. Quite rightly, he warned against outright disclosure at that time. A century beforehand, Paracelsus held forth a similar view:

> . . . the imagination of the majority of men and women at the present state of civilisation is too weak, their will too feeble, and their faith too much pervaded by doubt, to produce the desired effects; and it is fortunate that their imagination, however evil it may be, has not much power as long as the state of morality is not higher advanced than it is at present.

Much the same can be said of our present era, in which the knowledge of positive thinking is available to all, yet not fully understood, and often misused. As with the jungle witch-doctors of old, the modern practitioner of positive thinking has it within his power to kill or cure, should success with the process be attained. Years of steady progress in medical research has established that the human body functions by means of chemical reaction instituted by electro-agnetic impulses sent through the nerves from the subconscious area of the brain. The system is entirely involuntary in that the reasoning powers of the conscious mind play no part in its implementation. The conscious mind, however, can and does interfere with the process, emotional stress causing internal ailments such as asthma or, at the worst, cancer. Devote some analytical thought to the concept of emotional stress and it will be discovered that it causes conflict between that which the conscious mind believes and beliefs held by the subconscious.

As Emile Coué has unequivocally stated, the subconscious will dominate in every instance, the result of the conflict being borne by the physical body.

In recent times considerable publicity has been given to 'alternative' medicine, and the fact that it is looked upon with disfavour by orthodox medical men. The latter place their faith in a clinically prepared drug which has evolved after a period of laboratory research, rather than a mild extract from a flower, a root, or the bark of a tree. Those who advocate alternative medicine, however, fervently believe that drug company products do far more harm than good, and place unqualified trust in 'natural' remedies. What both factions completely fail to recognise is that neither laboratory drugs nor natural remedy should be prescribed without taking some account of the patient's belief in one or the other. As long as orthodox doctors don't believe in the curative powers of alternative medicines, the results of their investigative research into them will inevitably be of a negative nature. They cannot seem to grasp the fact that it is necessary to *believe* in order to obtain a successful, curative result.

It is imperative to realise that our whole journey through life is governed by the manner in which we individually and collectively, either consciously or unconsciously, exercise the power of Belief. Every superstition you care to name has this principle as its foundation, from those of the Aboriginal who 'points the bone' and attempts to sing his enemy to death, from those of the voodoo practitioner who sticks pins in a doll, down to the less drastic habit of wearing a St Christopher medallion as a good luck charm. If a man carries a rabbit's foot in the belief that it will bring him luck, then it will – so long as his belief reaches his subconscious in the necessary manner. But it is the Belief that does the work, not the rabbit's foot. Equally, if a man inadvertently walks under a ladder and regrets doing so because he believes it will bring bad luck, then should his belief in this ridiculous superstition reach his subconscious, bad luck will indeed be his lot. It is not the ladder which causes his luck to turn, it is himself and his lack of understanding in regard to his own mental powers.

An outstanding modern-day example of the power of positive thinking was that exercised by the boxer, Cassius

Clay – later Mohammed Ali. Every boxing fan will recall his ultra-positive attitude, with the cry of 'I am the greatest!'. As the idea of a rabbit's foot acts as a catalyst in the example above, so Clay's change of religion and adoption of the name Mohammed Ali did the same, acting as a foundation on which to support his change of belief. With the conviction that his new God was supporting him, and aided by the repetition of a positive phrase, Ali did indeed become just what he wanted to be.

As the glare of the sporting spotlight does not shine on all, many cases of successful positive thinking remain private affairs. More often than not, individuals invoke the great power of the subconscious without realising they are doing so, sometimes with beneficial results, at others with disastrous effects, as the following true accounts exemplify.

Some years ago the television series, *Strange Powers*, presented by science and fiction writer Arthur C. Clarke, investigated a seemingly unexplainable tide of events which overtook a family in Hexham, Northumberland. The family suffered the traumatic loss of two daughters, killed in a road accident. When the wife announced some time later that she was pregnant, the husband became utterly convinced that she would give birth to twin daughters and that they would be reincarnations of their dead children. Indeed, twin girls were born. One had a scar on her face and a thumb-shaped birthmark on her hip, blemishes identical to those carried by her dead predecessor. As the twins grew up and were able to talk, they displayed knowledge of places frequented by the dead girls, but which they themselves had not yet seen. No one could explain this mystery – no one, that is, who did not understand that the husband, in his grief, projected to his subconscious a strong *conviction* that his lost daughters would be reincarnated. So powerful and positive was this belief that it successfully impregnated the subconscious, and the collective subconscious, which can work miracles, acted accordingly. The mechanics of the concept of reincarnation and how it was achieved in this case will be more fully discussed in a later chapter.

Less fortunate was Spanish hotel executive Jaime Castell, of Barcelona. In late February 1979, he visited an insurance company to take out a policy on his life. Castell was quite explicit about the kind of insurance he needed – £50,000, payable to his pregnant wife and three year old son, with no benefits while he lived. A few weeks previously, Castell went on to explain, he had dreamed of a voice which told him that he would never live to see his unborn child, due in three months. He had become totally convinced that the dream would come true. Naturally suspicious, the insurance company ordered an exhaustive medical check, only to receive a report stating that the subject was 'an exceptional example of a healthy 30 year old man'. An investigation into Castell's private life only revealed that he was 'extremely conscientious, sober, a non-smoker, careful in every way, with no dangerous habits or hobbies'. Nevertheless still suspicious, the insurance company manager warned Jaime that there were certain circumstances that would invalidate the claim. Castell hastened to assure him that he was not contemplating suicide.

> 'I am a devout Catholic,' he said, 'and I dearly want to live . . . but I won't.'

In mid-March, with the policy granted and the premium paid, Castell was driving at a steady fifty miles an hour to his home on the outskirts of Barcelona. Another car, travelling in the opposite direction at more than a hundred miles an hour, suddenly went out of control at the precise moment the two cars occupied the same stretch of road. Hitting the safety barrier which divided the motorway, it somersaulted and crashed down on the top of Jaime's car. Both drivers were killed instantly.

The insurance company paid without question, for as their representative pointed out:

> 'This incredible accident rules out any suspicion. A fraction of a second either way and Castell would have escaped the somersaulting car.'

To the reader who has no knowledge of the magnitude of the Hermetic scheme, it would appear impossible that Castell successfully wished his own death. Nevertheless, it is a fact that the same power which saved Steve Hoholik by transmitting an impulse to the matrix of the collective subconscious, reacted to Castell's strength of *conviction* – his unshakeable belief – and manoeuvred events accordingly. Castell brought about his own demise as surely as if he had physically committed suicide. The fact that Jaime, in his conscious mind's thinking, dearly wished to continue living, counted for nothing as long as his *knowing* that he would die was the stronger emotion. It was Paracelsus who said that

> . . . the will creates forces that have nothing to do with reason, but obey blindly.

The natural evolution of existing mankind, from birth to adulthood, is such that it is inherent within us to be totally ignorant of the self-contained power which the exercise of Belief can invoke – unless either a revelation is experienced, or a teacher is successful in overcoming the great barriers of preconception and ingrained prejudice. Teaching can only help if the novice himself is prepared to adjust mentally, while a revelation is only likely to be forthcoming after a prolonged period of intense study of the subject.

Visualise the collective sub-conscious as a vast network of electrical force, an electro-magnetic field to which we are all mentally connected, and which may be termed the Matrix. From our limited point of view, we can only properly comprehend the Matrix as a blind force waiting to be activated by individual application of the power of Belief, by way of positive thinking, for the governing energy to which the Matrix responds is Certainty. From the Matrix emanate the impulses which impel every human being through his or her daily life; and the development of the feeling of 'knowing' within us is the only way in which we may consciously return impulses to it. If the individual does not master the art of positive thinking in its entirety, he will only ever be able to return impulses to it in an involuntary manner as is normally the case, and thus will not be able to mould its forces to his own will, a fact that philosophers of the past have tried to instil into us on more than one occasion. The 16th century alchemist, Jean Baptiste van Helmont, in his work, *Opera Omnia*, plainly stated that

> . . . the will of the Creator, through which all things

were made and received their first impulse, is the property of every living being. Man, endowed with an additional spirituality, has the largest share of it on this planet. It depends on the proportion of the matter in him whether he will exercise its magical faculty with more or less success. Sharing this divine potency in common with every inorganic atom, he exercises it through the course of his whole life, whether consciously or otherwise. In the former case, when in full possession of his powers, he will be the master, and the *magnale magnum* will be controlled and guided by him. . . .

In this passage, the Matrix is represented by *magnale magnum*, a Latin name favoured by mediaeval alchemists. There have been many alternatives, however, with Eliphas Levi referring to it as the *Astral Light*, 'man's reflective mirror', while earlier philosophers listed a hundred different names for it, including *The Primal Matter; Sulpher; Quicksilver;* or *Mercury of the Sages.* The general mass of uninitiated people of both past and present know it as *God; The Lord; Father; Fate; Destiny* or *Providence.*

Emile Coué, brief and to the point, reaffirms the teaching of van Helmont when he writes:

This principle is the property of everyone from birth to death and we play with it unconsciously all our lives. ·

Belief, the active force of mind applied in positive thinking, was named by the old philosophers only in an ambiguous manner such as I have already revealed. It was far more likely to find them tantalising readers with descriptions like that offered by Robert Valens Rugl, in his 17th century text, *The Glory of The World*:

. . . for the matter is only one thing, and would remain one thing, though a hundred thousand books had been written about it. . . . It is familiar to all men, both young and old, is found in the country, in the village, in the town, in all things created by God; yet it is despised by all. Rich and poor handle it every day. It is cast into the street by serving maids. Children play with it. Yet no one prizes it, though, next to the human soul, it is the most beautiful and the most precious thing on earth, and has the power to pull down kings and princes. Nevertheless, it is esteemed the vilest and meanest of earthly things. It is cast away and rejected by all. Indeed, it is the Stone which the builders of Solomon disallowed. But if it be prepared in the right way, it is a pearl without price and, indeed, an earthly anti-type of Christ, the heavenly Corner Stone.

Yes, the literary ploys with which the Hermetic writers sought to convey the concept of Belief's magical power were numerous and varied. As an alternative example, let us briefly examine a text of the 1620s – *Labyrinth of the World and the Paradise of the Heart*. The writer, whose real name was Johann Amos Komensky, but who employed the Latinized pseudonym Comenius, was greatly influenced by a contemporary, the Rosicrucian Johann Valentin Andreae, Grand Master of the Priory of Sion. The main theme of Comenius's work is the Labyrinth itself, a great city where, in contrast to Utopia and other mystical cities of literature, everything is wrong and all man's endeavour is futile, leading to nothing. In chapter twelve, in a direct parody of the Rosicrucian Furore, the author describes the arrival of a herald who tells the citizens of a band of wise men who had remedied the insufficiencies of the world. To make gold, he said, was one of the smallest of their hundred feats, for all Nature was bared and revealed to them. The news was received in various ways – some overjoyed, others dubious or frightened – and there ensued a great debate as to the truth of what the messenger had said. Meanwhile, another visitor to the city had arrived, a trader offering 'wondrous secrets' said to be taken from the treasury of this new philosophy. Everything that was sold was wrapped up in boxes that were painted and emblazoned with various Latin inscriptions. The purchasers were forbidden to open their boxes, for it was said that the force of the secret wisdom was such that it worked by penetrating the cover, but if the box was opened, it would evaporate and vanish. Some complied with the dictate, but others more bold could not refrain from opening them and, finding them completely empty, showed this to the rest, who thereupon opened theirs. But no one found anything.

> Then they cried, 'Fraud, fraud!' and spoke furiously to
> him who had sold the wares, but he calmed them saying
> that these were the most secret of secret things, and that
> they were invisible to all but 'Filiae scientae' (that is, the
> sons of science). . . .

The point of this quaint and slightly comic fable is to
exemplify the need for Faith (Belief). Had the owners of the
boxes believed strongly enough in the power of the secret
within, then they would have been practising the art of
positive thinking.

One of the best known and most often quoted of Hermetic
documents from even earlier times is the famous Smagdarina,
the Emerald Tablets of Hermes, which in a few sentences is
said to contain the whole essence of Hermetic wisdom. There
are, as may be expected considering its great age, slight
variations in different translations, but the fundamental
message has survived remarkably unchanged. It is only the
first sentence which holds our interest in this work. It begins

> True, no lie, certain, and without doubt,. . . .

You will notice that in this opening line, the factor of
Certainty is placed before the reader's eyes not once, but *four*
times. Right from the very beginning, therefore, the whole
secret is given, provided there is the wit to understand it. And
if you recall my comments regarding the Hermetic colours at
the beginning of chapter one, you will also understand that the
figure *four* was used by the early philosophers, from whose era
the Emerald Tablets originate, to denote by colour the four
stages of the mental process.

Even more fleeting as a clue, but equally infallible as a guide,
are those sentences in philosophic texts, including the Bible,
which contain the phrases 'a certain man', or 'a certain place'.
Ordinarily perceived by the reader to be reference to a
particular man, or place, the secret intent is to direct attention
to a positive thinker, or to the mind, the place where positive
thinking is carried out. The Bible texts, apart from containing
veritable masterpieces of allegorical invention, are amazingly
liberal, with open references to the application of Faith/Belief,
but owing to the misleading indoctrination by the Church,
few are able to interpret them in the correct manner. True, the

Clergy have always advised the members of their flock to 'have faith in God', but lacking the true understanding of what 'God' actually is, such faith is consistently misdirected and is therefore of little or no benefit to the individual. The great error lies in the personalisation of 'God', as a 'He', as 'our Father who art in heaven', as the all-seeing One who looks down on our every deed, good or bad. As I have attempted to show, 'God' is our own subconscious power, available to us if we make contact in the right way, without the need of a human minister, let alone one who himself prays in ignorance. The Christian 'God' is not a 'He', nor a 'She', but an IT, and should be comprehended as an impersonal Force which is at our disposal, providing we can modify our thinking sufficiently so as to allow inlet to it. Thus, Christian prayer will only be answered by successful positive thinking, the correct use of Faith. With this in mind, let us examine a typical story line from the Gospel:

Matt. 9,

27. And when Jesus departed thence, two blind men followed him crying and saying; Thou son of David, have mercy on us.

28. And when he was come into the house, the blind men came to him; and Jesus saith unto them, Believe ye that I am able to do this? They said unto him Yea, Lord.

29. Then touched he their eyes, saying, According to your faith be it unto you.

30. And their eyes were opened. . . .

In this anecdote, the character Jesus is portrayed as a faith healer by reputation and it is made clear that the blind men *believe* in his power to work healing miracles, but just to be absolutely sure of this, Jesus is made to ask them outright; 'Do you believe that I am able to restore your sight? And they replied that they did. Jesus then touched their eyes, saying; 'According to *your* faith, be it unto you.' (By the power of your own belief you have healed yourselves).

The power to heal, either oneself or others, lies within each and every mind, requiring only a developed sense of positive thinking for it to manifest. If this were not so, there would be no faith healers in the world, either at the time the

Gospels were written or at the present. And perhaps this analysis may throw some light on the puzzling question of why some of the sick cannot be cured by the faith healer. The fault is not necessarily with the healer, but with the unbelieving patient.

The fundamentalist churchgoer, even of the enlightened present, makes the mistake of believing in a God external to him, and never being able to make contact with such an abstraction, places his trust instead in the ministers of the Church, believing them to be the closest representative of God. Hence, the structure of the Church, from the Pope downwards, is supported by a belief to which it has no real claim. Many Gnostics have made reference to this fundamentalist folly, and if an example is required, what better or more clearly stated than the passages to be found in Jocob Boehme's *Theosophical Works, Book Three* (of Regeneration, or the New Birth).

137. What good end doth it answer for me to go to the material churches of stone, and there fill my ears with empty breath?

151. . . . But Babel (the uninitiated masses) hath a heap of stones into which she goeth in fine clothes with her seeming holiness and real hypocrisy. There she loveth to be seen in fine clothes, and maketh a very devout and goodly show; the church of stone is her God, in which she putteth her confidence.

152. But the holy man hath his church about him everywhere, even in himself; for he always standeth and walketh, sitteth and lieth down in his church. He liveth in the true Christian Church; yea, in the temple of Christ. . . .

This message from a 16th century philosopher is quite clear – the God you are seeking is in yourself, not in the structure or the ministers of the Church. Carl Jung, that knowledgeable philosopher of our own time, came to the same conclusion, as is evident from this passage in *Mysterium Conjunctionis* (Vol. 14, Collected Works):

. . . the Church can never explain the truth of her images because she acknowledges no point of view but her own. She moves solely within the framwork of her images and her argument must always beg the question. The flock of harmless sheep was ever the symbolic prototype of the credulous crowd, though the Church is quick to recognise the wolves in sheep's clothing who lead the faith of the multitude astray in order to destroy them. The tragedy is that the blind trust which leads to perdition is practised just as much inside the Church and is praised as the highest virtue. . . .

Another commentator on this subject, as knowledgeable as Jung but held in much less esteem by academics, is Madame Blavatsky, a founder in 1875 of the Theosophical Society, the teachings of which have made a profound impact upon religious thought in the West. Towards the end of her life, she edited a magazine entitled *Lucifer* (meaning 'light', that is, understanding), wherein she answered questions sent in by subscribers. Here is one of her replies to a particular theme:

> The 'coming of Christ' means the presence of *Christos* in a regenerated world, and not at all the actual coming in body of 'Christ' Jesus. This Christ is to be sought neither in the wilderness nor 'in the inner chambers', nor in the sanctuary of any temple or church built by man; for Christ – the true esoteric SAVIOUR – is no man, but the DIVINE PRINCIPLE in every human being.

In case this is not lucid enough, she elsewhere quotes Chaucer's words:

> Faith is the key of Christendom.

In our present era, Norman Vincent Peale offers a tremendously revealing passage in *The Power Of Positive Thinking*, when he admits that

> I read the Bible for years before it dawned on me that it was trying to tell me that if I would have faith – and really have it – I could overcome all my difficulties, meet every situation, rise above every defeat and solve all the perplexing problems of my life. . . .

In other words, Peale stopped believing in the abstraction of an external God and started to believe instead in the power of Faith (Belief). Only by doing so did he achieve results. In this, witness the unwitting change of an ordinary fundamentalist into a true Gnostic. And with this observation, we are well on our way towards an understanding of the phrase so often applied in *Hermes Unveiled*, the 'transmission of the consciousness'. Such a transmission is, in fact, an expansion of the faculty of understanding to a point well beyond average boundaries, and it may be that the best possible description of such a highly desirable maturing of the mind can be gleaned from the experiences of Richard Maurice Bucke, M.D. author of *Cosmic Consciousness* (1901).

At the age of 36, Bucke had spent an early spring evening in the company of two friends, discussing classical literature. At midnight, he took his leave and began the journey back to his home. Sitting in the hansom cab, he was in a state of quiet enjoyment as he thought back on the evening's agreeable chit-chat. Suddenly, with no warning at all, he found himself

> . . . wrapped around as it were by a flame coloured cloud.

For the first brief instant he thought that there was a fire close by, but in the next second knew that the illusion of light was in his own mind. There immediately followed what he describes as a sense of exultation, a feeling of immense joyousness, culminating in an intellectual illumination that he finds impossible to put adequately into words. He 'saw' and knew that the Cosmos is not dead matter but a living Presence, that the soul of man is immortal, that the universe is built and operated so that all things work together for the good of each and all, that the foundation principle of the world is what we call love, and that the happiness of everyone is in the long run absolutely certain. He learned more within the few seconds during which the illumination lasted than in years of previous study, and indeed, much more than any amount of study could have disclosed to him. Although brief, the illumination was so vivid that it became impossible for him to forget what he had understood because of it. The supreme occurrence of that night, he wrote, was his real initiation into a *new and higher order of ideas*.

As a result of this revelation, Bucke later outlined the stages of human consciousness, separating them into four. They are

1. Minimal perception, as that of an amoeba.
2. Simple consciousness – to be conscious of all things material which surround one, but not to be conscious of oneself, i.e. as an animal, with all attention directed outwards, with no analytical self-perception.
3. Self Consciousness – to be conscious not only of all which surrounds one, but also to be aware of oneself. To be able to self-analyse – as intelligent man can do at this stage of his development.
4. Cosmic Consciousness – the development of intuitional understanding. To become aware of a much wider, previously unperceived order of things, not by seeing them with the senses, but by KNOWING them with the understanding.

Thus, the 'transmission of consciousness' undertaken by the Hermetic initiates is the act of moving from step three to step four of Bucke's chart. And it must be emphatically stated here that such a transition, despite its allegorical description of upheaval such as an 'earthquake' or a 'violent storm', does not mean a disassociation of mind, or a mental disorientation of the kind that may be induced by a sudden and powerful shock, or by drugs. Neither is it trance, ecstasy or mediumship, or the mind in any state of limbo, as imagined by occult fiction writers. As it is primarily an expansion of the understanding and intuition, it can best be summed up as a greatly modified attitude of mind, brought about by being freed from the constraints of a lifetime's misconceptions. One feature of such an illumination is that, although it does not alter the person in physical appearance, there is an added magnetism, or charm, to the personality, brought into being without apparent effort on the part of the subject. This takes place purely on a mental level, not as the result of an outward, ingratiatory demeanour.

Not every initiate is blessed with an instant revelation as experienced by Bucke. More often than not, step four is attained only after many years of study in which the mind is made to ponder the secrets of philosophy and the various religions, until at last a breakthrough comes, or the wisdom is imparted piece by piece.

Further, such revelatory experiences are not confined to an

emergence through the study of philosophy or religion alone. Albert Einstein, for instance, was hardly seen by the rest of the world as a Gnostic philosopher, but when a Rabbi wrote to him explaining that he had sought in vain to comfort his daughter over the death of her sister, Einstein replied thus:

> A human being is part of the whole called by us 'Universe', a part limited in time and space. He experiences himself, his thoughts and feelings, as something separated from the rest – a kind of optical delusion of his consciousness. This delusion is a kind of prison for us, restricting us to our personal desires and to affection for a few people nearest to us. Our task must be to free ourselves from this prison by widening our circle of compassion to embrace all living creatures and the whole of nature in its beauty. Nobody is able to achieve this completely, but the striving for such an achievement is in itself a part of the liberation and a foundation for inner security.

It is perfectly clear, from the content of this passage, that Einstein had developed his own Hermetic understanding in close relationship with his theoretical knowledge of Time and Space. For the lay person to appreciate this, it is only necessary for them to link the 'Universe' of Einstein with the remarks made by Austin O. Spare about the Butterfly. The 'I' of the Butterfly, of the human, and of the Universe are one and the same.

Hermetic use of the visualisation technique advocated by Norman Peale – that is, prayerise; picturise; actualise – was seldom touched upon by mediaeval scribes, or written about in a manner that could be readily understood. Yet it is a fact that the earliest of the Old Testament texts gave an analogy so near to the truth that many of the older philosophers were uneasy to know that the general public had it so close to hand. I refer to the story of Jacob, with his speckled and ringstraked cattle, as described in Genesis chapter 30, verses 31 to 43. Previously, I have described and disclosed in detail the allegorical meaning of Jacob and his Ladder (Genesis 28, 11 to 18 – *Hermes Unveiled*, page 96), and therefore in interpreting the story of his cattle we must continue to be aware that 'Jacob' is not a real, historical person, but a characterisation intended to represent an Hermetic initiate (positive thinker). As Bibles are generally ready to hand, I feel no need to duplicate the verses here, but instead will turn immediately to *Bring Out The Magic In Your Mind*, and let Al Koran put the interpretation into plain language

> The oldest story of visualisation comes from the Bible –
> that of Jacob and the spotted cattle. He cut little bits of
> round bark off trees and laid these pieces at the bottom of
> a clear stream where the cattle drank. Every time the
> beasts looked into the water they visualised these spots
> and their offspring brought Jacob his desired spotted
> cattle.

To slightly enlarge upon it, the cattle saw themselves in the water, but as spotted cattle, owing to the presence of the round pieces of bark. Thus they conceived of themselves as spotted, a fixated idea (*knowing*) that transferred itself to their calves. I repeat that this incident did not take place in reality. It is intended to be analogous of the process where the conscious mind (the cattle) pictures something in its imagination (gazes into the reflection in the *water*) and then waits for it to materialise in reality (the spotted calves are born).

Chapter Four

I cannot emphasise enough the fact that manifestation of the subconscious power occurs time and time again without the recipients being aware of the true nature of the phenomenon. Its effect creates enduring mysteries with which to baffle those unable to understand what is happening simply because the scale of the manifestation is beyond the level of acceptable credibility. What is the level of acceptable credibility but the restrictive boundaries imposed by prejudice, or defined by material knowledge gained through scientific experiment alone? Science in the laboratory has never taken account of the power of Belief, or its effect upon human beings and their surroundings, and has thus alienated itself from the most potent aspect of experiment. The truth of this statement will be upheld by an examination of the work of such pioneers as George de la Warr, or Curtis F. Upton, but let us begin with a mystery that has fascinated one and all for nearly a hundred years – the saga of John Worrel Keely.

With the exception of the recorded fact that Keely was born in Philadelphia, USA, in 1827, data concerning his early years is sparse, but he appears to have reached manhood as a jack-of-all-trades, a carpenter, a musician, and an illusionist specialising in card tricks. For a period, he was even a trapper in the Rocky Mountains. It was while engaged in the latter, rugged occupation that he became involved in a skirmish with Indians, sustaining a severe wound from an arrow. As soon as he was fit enough to resume travel, he returned to his home town to convalesce, afterwards settling down and acquiring an engineering workshop so that he might experiment with his own inventions. It was not until 1871 that his name began to excite interest, for in this period he suddenly announced the discovery of a powerful new form of energy. Industry, at that particular state of its evolution, had already realised that the established methods of producing power would soon be insufficient to sustain growth. With the work of Faraday,

Ohm, Clerk–Maxwell and others, there was a mounting expectation that electro-motive power would soon replace steam, water and coal. Consequently, when Keely declared his discovery, there was immediate interest.

In his workshop the inventor had constructed, among other things, a strange machine that was capable of bending steel rails and tearing giant hawsers to shreds with a force which far exceeded anything in use at the time. But when asked to explain how such energy was generated, he described his 'motor' as a 'device which disintegrated the etheric force which controls the automatic constitution of matter'. His engines, he maintained, operated on 'harmonic vibration'.

Scientists and engineers may have expressed scepticism, but by his demonstrations Keely managed to gather about him a number of enthusiastic, if somewhat bewildered, investors who were willing to finance further experiments in the hope that the mysterious force could be applied commercially. In 1879, they gathered together in his workshop to witness the 'motor' drive a nine inch steel ball through the air with such force that it completely penetrated two thick oaken planks before burying itself in a sandbox at the far end of the room. For nearly ten years, Keely pursued similar experiments in his attempts to isolate and harness the mysterious force, by which time his stockholders had lost their patience. During one stormy meeting in 1882 Keely eventually agreed to meet any academic representative that the investors cared to select and show him the 'motor'. A candidate of suitable standing was nominated, subsequently reporting that although he didn't understand the exact nature of the force which powered the machine, there was no doubt at all that Keely had indeed discovered all he claimed. As to how the force could be successfully harnessed for commercial use, he added, that was something he was unable to answer.

On those terms, Keely managed to keep his enterprise going for a further six years, but matters finally came to a head in 1888 when the investors, by now convinced that he was either a fraud or was deliberately holding back his secret, took him to court. When Keely was directed by the judge to reveal the details of his motive force, he either would not, or could not, with the result that he was imprisoned. Angry stockholders broke into his workshop, all but wrecking it in an attempt to discover how the 'motor' operated, but all they found was a large metal sphere containing compressed air. There was nothing secret, or exceptional about that, for Keely had openly displayed it on previous occasions, and in any case, everyone agreed that the pipes attached to it were inadequate to carry the pressure that would have been required to energise the machine. All the witnesses of the previous demonstrations could agree upon was that the machine made a 'humming sound'.

That is the story as it is generally known, and from that time to this, interested historians have posed the same questions; did Keely really discover a mysterious force, and if so, of what nature could it have been – electrical, magnetic, or was it something entirely revolutionary to science? Or was the whole episode no more than a drawn out confidence trick, a grand charade that might well have been conceived and perpetrated by a part time magician?

After serving his sentence, and up until the time of his death in 1898, Keely was financed by a wealthy Philadelphian widow, Mrs Bloomfield-Moore, and it was due to her patronage that pamphlets were published in which Keely attempted to justify his extraordinary discovery, and to explain it. It must be noted, however, that the texts did little towards acceptance of his theories by the scientific fraternity of the day. In one reference work, Keely writes:

> My engine has neither pistons nor eccentrics, nor is there one grain of pressure exerted in the engine, whatever may be the size and capacity of it. My system, in every part and detail, both in the developing of my power and in every branch of its utilisation, is based and founded on sympathetic vibration.

The problem lay, of course, in the exact interpretation of Keely's phrase, 'sympathetic vibration'. Elsewhere, he tried another approach:

> In the conception of my vibratory engine, I did not seek to obtain perpetual motion, but a circuit is formed that actually has a neutral centre, which is in a condition to be vivified by my vibratory ether.

Further questions, therefore, are; what is 'vibratory ether', and what is a 'neutral centre'? To describe the latter, Keely asks his readers to imagine a planet of some 20,000 miles in diameter during its early stages of formation, but the matter of which, instead of coalescing into a sphere of solid rock, separated into a small inner sphere enclosed within a large outer ball, but with a void in between. He points out that if the inner sphere was the size of a billiard ball and the outer crust was some 5,000 miles thick, their respective gravitational masses would cancel each other out and thus they would remain, perfectly balanced. This is what he termed a 'neutral centre'.

By 'vibratory ether', Keely most certainly meant 'thought-power', for elsewhere he had written that

> . . . the action of the mind is a vibratory etheric evolution, controlling the physical, its negative power being depreciatory in its effects and its positive influence elevation.

You will have noticed that with this statement, we have returned to the basic principle of positive thinking – Certainty and Doubt. It is clear, then, that Keely was endeavouring to convey the rather impossible idea that his machine was operated by thought-power, and it is hardly surprising that the claim found no favour with orthodox scientific circles of the day. But others held a different view. In 1876, when the renowned Madame Blavatsky visited the Philadelphia Centennial Exhibition, she was approached by an admirer of Keely's work and asked for her opinion of the inventor and his elusive 'force'. She replied that those more versed in occult knowledge than herself had stated that the inventor of the Self-Motor was a 'natural born magician' i.e. endowed with supernormal mental power; that he would continue to be unconscious of the full range of the power and would employ only that which he had stumbled upon – firstly, because attributing it to the wrong source, he would never be able to invoke further power; and secondly, because it was beyond him to pass to others a power that was his alone. Madame Blavatsky also related the story about one of Keely's stockholders who, desperate to uncover the inventor's secret, managed to get an investigator into Keely's workforce to spy on him. After six months of close watching, the man suddenly blurted out to Keely that he knew how it was done. They had been setting up a machine together and Keely was manipulating the control, which turned the force on and off. At the man's declaration, Keely stepped back and gestured at the control.

'Try it, then,' he said.

The man turned the control, confidently – but nothing happened.

'Let me see you do it once more,' the investigator asked, and Keely obliged. As soon as he turned the control, the force manifested. Once more they changed places and the investigator operated the control, but still with no result. Then Keely placed his hand on the man's shoulder.

'Now try it,' he ordered. The investigator did so, and the force was instantaneously invoked.

During his many years of experimental research, there is no doubt that Keely produced some remarkable effects, one aspect of which involved the use of sound waves – perhaps the commencement of his investigation into 'sympathetic vibration'. He began with the production of certain tones obtained by drawing a violin bow over a tuning fork, or by playing a chord on his violin. These he called 'etheric vibrations'. The result of this particular line of research culminated in demonstrations cᶠ how the force of gravity could be overcome. According to his notes, he used a model airship weighing about 8 lbs, to which was attached a platinum and silver wire leading to a transmitter of sympathetic vibrations. As specific tones were sounded in the transmitter, the airship rose, descended, or hovered in mid-air, 'swaying gently, like a piece of thistledown.' From a six feet long 'generator', a product of early experimentation, Keely managed to obtain the same effect from a device no larger than an old fashioned pocket watch and which, according to one report, generated a pressure of force said to have been measured at 30,000 lbs.

A phenomenon of a similar kind was the subject of a chapter in Ostrander and Schroeder's *Psychic Discoveries Behind The Iron Curtain* (1970). Therein the authors describe the work of

Robert Pavlita, a Czechoslovakian businessman who, in the 1940s, began a thirty-year period of research into development of what he calls 'psychic generators'. The functions of these so-called generators vary according to their shape, each one being activated by Pavlita, who claims that they pick up bio-energy from his as he stares at them.

Pavlita's rather unusual research came to the attention of the general public some time before the Russians invaded Czechoslovakia, after an English journalist wrote an article detailing the astounding principle of the generators. The Czechoslovakian newspapers took up the story, causing an overnight sensation, much to the displeasure of the government of the day, who immediately forbade further publicity and then directed a group of scientists to make a thorough investigation. By the time Ostrander and Schroeder arrived in Prague to witness demonstrations of the 'psychotronic generators', as they were now called, more than seventy had been designed by Pavlita, all of which were being enthusiastically experimented with by a commission of scholars from the Academy of Science and the University of Hradec Králové. Of the examples quoted in the book, one is described as a chunky metal doughnut with a slice through one side. The metal circlet was supported on a rod with a base, the whole looking like a shaving mirror. The authors were told that if flies were placed in this generator, they died instantly. They were also shown film of another generator at work on what was hoped to be a practical application of the discovery. Sealed bottles of polluted water from a textile factory were irradiated by a generator for twelve hours, after which the water was seen to be clear, the pollutant crystalized and fallen to the bottom of the bottles. It was claimed that such purification could not have been carried out by a chemical purifier. Astutely, the authors equate this experiment with those undertaken in America in which scientists had examined water in a sealed flask that had been held in the hands of a faith healer. It was found that a molecular change in the water had taken place, a spreading of the bonds between hydrogen and oxygen atoms. Such is the power of Faith (Belief).

According to Ostrander and Schroeder, at the time of

writing, Pavlita – like the unfortunate Keely – had not been able to apply his 'psychotronic generators' in a practical manner.

The principle behind both experimenters is that of Belief, and the energy which it can sometimes cause to be manifested, if conditions are right. The lives of Keely and Pavlita have similarities in that they both spent many years with their minds focussed on research which they *believed* would produce results, and both men were able to produce within themselves sufficient *conviction* which resulted in the subconscious power being involuntarily invoked within them. What led Keely to begin his experiments with sound waves and to eventually study the theosophic aspect of physics is not recorded, but Pavlita, when asked how he had come to embark upon such a bizarre enterprise, replied briefly that it was because he studied many 'old texts'. It is said that history repeats itself, and certainly the strange case of John Keely has its modern counterpart in the spoon-bending saga of Uri Geller. The constant attempts by newspaper reporters and theatrical magicians to discredit Geller's claim that his metal-bending ability is of a paranormal nature, are a familiar chapter in the present era's supernormal casebook. Uppermost in the list of questions provoked by the Geller phenomenon is that which asks; if he can bend spoons, forks and keys by paranormal means, why is such phenomena not employed in a more useful manner? Why, indeed, the ghost of Keely would ask with irony.

In deciding how to formulate an answer to this tricky question, non-initiate observers would need to be acquainted with Uri Geller's performance at first hand but it may suffice here to review an incident which embodies most of the conditions demanded by sceptics, and in fact was conducted by a journalist intent on 'exposing' the Israeli for the sleight of hand technician many believe him to be. In January 1974 Geller made one of his periodic visits to England to fulfil a cabaret contract, and *Daily Express* reporter, Don Coolican, was detailed to cover the artist's visit, and to obtain evidence that made a lie of the claim to paranormalcy, if possible. Subsequently, two articles appeared in the *Express*, on the 25th and 26th respectively, giving biographical details about Geller and hints as to how his paranormal tricks could be detected as illusions. Determined to challenge the Israeli, Coolican had been briefed by leading members of the Magic Circle on how to bend spoons, twist forks and snap keys with the aid of sleight of hand and a chemical formula. Theatrical magicians had told Coolican that they knew exactly how Geller performed his feats and demonstrated that they could duplicate them by means of their magic art.

Armed with this knowledge, the reporter followed Geller to his next appearance in Copenhagen, there to face him with accusations of trickery. An arrangement was made for Uri to come to Coolican's hotel room where, in company of reporter Andrew Fyall and photographer Harry Dempster, the Israeli was to be subjected to a test calculated to disprove once and for all his claim to paranormal powers. On arrival at the room, a place where there was no chance of apparatus being prearranged, Geller immediately took off his jacket and permitted the reporters to search him for hidden objects. When this had been completed to the reporters' satisfaction, the Israeli emptied all of his pockets. Then he rolled up his sleeves and thoroughly washed his hands so that he could not be accused of using chemicals which may be adhering to his fingers.

'Unless the tap water had changed to some chemical fluid,' Coolican later wrote, 'his hands were then spotless.'

During these preparations, all three newspapermen were watching closely, but detected not the faintest suspicion of a covert move. What happened next is best described by Andrew Fyall:

> I selected the thickest, longest and strongest key in my pocket – an A.A. members' key – and invited Uri to bend it without it ever leaving my hand. We stood near a hotel room window beside a metal radiator grill (Uri said it helped to be close to other metal objects) and he stroked the tip of the silver-coloured key, while I held the diamond-shaped head in between my right forefinger and thumb. 'I'm willing it to bend,' he said. He stroked the key gently between his own forefinger and thumb, occasionally only with his forefinger, exerting no

appreciable pressure at all. If I had released my hold on the key it would have fallen to the floor. It took about twenty seconds for the key to start bending. Slowly at first, then quite perceptibly, it bent upwards. 'I'm getting good results,' said Uri. 'I feel good today.' I never took my eyes off the key and at no time did it leave my grip. Finally, after about a minute, Uri stepped back triumphantly and even as he stood there, several feet away, the key continued to bend in my hand. . . . Hours later, in my pocket, I could still feel the key bending further. . . .

Later, Geller performed other metal-bending feats and then, after a moment's pause with his eyes closed, accurately described the living room in Harry Dempster's home in Essex, correctly identifying the colour of the carpets, positioning of the furniture, and then discussed a seascape painting hung on Dempster's wall. Finally, turning to Andrew Fyall, he told him that he had recently been involved in a bad experience concerning his car and a white animal. Fyall admitted that, six weeks previously, he had knocked down and killed a white cat near his home in Kent. 'Like myself,' Coolican wrote, 'neither Fyall nor Dempster had met Uri before.'

Geller himself has no explanation regarding his powers. He said:

I feel it must come from some external source. Perhaps everybody has got this within them, but it requires a certain power to trigger it off. . . .

It is accepted that a certain amount of trickery is employed in the performance of Geller's stage act, but then he is in showbusiness. To bend metal, however, he makes use of the same subconscious power which Keely discovered, although he is at a loss to understand why such power should be restricted to the mundane focus of its application, something over which he has no control. In the cases of all three subjects, Keely, Pavlita and Geller, each successfully but involuntarily impregnated their own subconscious minds with the Certainty of an idea — and the subconscious inevitably reacted.

The same phenomenon manifests, generally unrecognised, in various other spheres of life. It is at least a century since the principle of homoeopathic medicine was placed before the public, yet still no one can offer a satisfactory explanation of the way in which it works. Orthodox medicine, while reluctantly admitting that its application will often result in a mysterious cure, remains sceptical, treating homoeopathy as a maverick science, a last resort, to be turned to only when long established procedures prove to be of no avail. Its unfathomable principle was chanced upon in the late 1770s by Christian Samuel Hahnemenn, a prominent physician of Meissen, Saxony. Also a chemist, a linguist and author of a comprehensive apothecaries' lexicon, Hahnemenn discovered the secret by accident while treating a patient for malaria. He found that the symptoms of the illness were relieved by an infusion of bark from a local tree – an infusion which, if administered to a person not suffering with malaria, would induce symptoms identical to it. Given to the malarial patient, however, it promptly effected a cure. Greatly mystified by this discovery, Hahnemenn sought out plants, herbs, barks, or any other substance, including snake venom, which could of themselves produce symptoms similar to those of a known disease in a healthy subject. By administering an essence of the substance to a sick patient, he achieved cures which bordered on the miraculous. Quite naturally, the good doctor wished to pass on this valuable knowledge for the benefit of suffering humanity and forthwith published his findings in the journal of Doctor Hufeland, personal physician to Goethe. Human prejudice being a predictable trait, it comes as no surprise to find that the Guild of Apothecaries, the pill-pushers of the time, looked upon the minute quantities of natural remedy prescribed by Hahnemenn as a threat to their profits. They used their influence to bring Hahnemenn to court where he was forbidden to dispense medicines and exiled from his native town.

Already paradoxical in principle, homoeopathic treatment is more so in view of the fact that the more the remedy is diluted, the stronger its effect seems to be, a state of affairs for which logical science can find no rational explanation.

Equally paradoxical is the principle behind the process

known as Radionics, a science which grew out of the discoveries of Dr Albert Abrams at the turn of the century – and, indeed, careful consideration may reveal a compatability between the two.

Son of a wealthy San Francisco merchant, Abrams studied advanced medicine at Heidelberg University before returning to the United States to teach Pathology. A master of the art of medical percussion, he would tap the bodies of his patients to produce resonances which guided him to a correct diagnosis of their afflications. One day, whilst working in close proximity to an X-ray machine, he noticed that whenever it was switched on, the resonances he got from his patient were unaccountably dull. Subsequent research revealed that the same dull sound that was induced by the X-ray field was to be found in a patient who suffered with cancer. In a further experiment, Abrams brought a boy into his classroom, stripped him to the waist and tapped his abdomen just above the navel, asking his students to note carefully the hollow, resonant quality of the sounding he was obtaining. He then asked one of his students to hold up a specimen of cancerous tissue to the boy's forehead, touching lightly for a few seconds, removing it, and then touching it again. While the student carried out these instructions, Abrams continued to percuss the boy's abdomen in the same place, and the class was amazed to hear that every time the tissue touched the boy's forehead, the percussed tone changed from fully resonant to dull. When Abrams substituted a specimen of tubercular tissue for the cancerous, and repeated the experiment, the tone did not change. But when he altered the position of the tapping to a point just below the navel, the effect reappeared. From these experiments, Abrams concluded that unknown waves of radiation emanating from the diseased specimens were being received by the boy's healthy body and that they were somehow causing a change in the character of the body tissue.

Eventually, this intriguing line of research led Abrams to state that the established concept that all disease was of cell-ular origin was wrong, and that disease occurs because the molecules of certain cells undergo a structural alteration which affects its atoms, changing the number and arrangement of their electrons. Only much later, when the characteristics have developed enough to affect a mass of cells does the imbalance become perceptible under a microscope. Exactly what force initiated the imbalance of the atoms, Abrams never knew, and even today no one has worked out a satisfactory solution to the problem, except for half-accepted ideas that stress – that is, emotional conflict – causes disharmony between the conscious and subconscious. Pursuing his theory, Abrams discovered that radiation from a pathological specimen could be transmitted through a wire like electricity, and he soon conceived a form of variable electrical oscillator, a machine that used radiation in place of electricity to emit sounds that would take the place of percussed tones, and with a dial from which diseases could be read according to the pitch of the tone. He called this machine a 'reflexophone', and later found it possible to diagnose the various ills of the human body by only a single drop of the patient's blood as a sample.

One day, in a strange duplication of Hahnemenn's work, Abrams was in his classroom demonstrating the reaction induced by a blood sample of a patient suffering with malaria. Of the students present, he asked why it was an accepted practise to treat a malarial patient with quinine. Could they, he wanted to know, give a scientific reason for the use of the essence? When there was no reply, he took a few grains of sulphate of quinine and placed them in the machine where the blood sample had been. All were astonished to see that it produced exactly the same percussion note as the blood sample. He then placed the malarial blood sample back in the machine, together with a grain or two of quinine wrapped in tissue paper. Astonishingly, the dull percussion note indicating malaria, changed to a resonant one indicating good health. To his amazed students, Abrams suggested that the radiations emitted by the quinine molecules exactly cancelled out those from the molecules of malarial blood sample, and that the effect by quinine on malaria was due to a *hitherto unsuspected electrical law*.

It must be patently obvious to the reader that the same unsuspected electrical law is the principle behind the homoeopathic discoveries of Dr Hahnemenn, and although this point of discussion may seem to be remote from the subject of positive thinking, it must be remembered that the active principle of Belief operates on the same atomic level as the radiations discovered by Abrams.

By 1919, Abrams had devised a radionic machine – an 'oscilloclast' – which could emit waves at variable frequencies, and which were capable of cancelling out radiations emitted by various diseases. Thus, the oscilloclast effectively duplicated, and took the place of, homoeopathic remedies.

Abrams died in 1924, and once again it is no revelation to find that his controversial research had aroused the prejudice of that pillar of orthodoxy, the American Medical Association, the representatives of which continued to vilify him after his death, denouncing him as a 'quack', and because of the unorthodox nature of circuit design in the 'Abrams Box', claiming that there was no other purpose in its manufacture than to make a quick financial killing at the expense of the gullible. The fact that Abrams was already a millionaire in his own right, and had offered to donate his machine to, and to work unremunerated, for any organisation which would develop his research in the interests of humanity, was completely ignored. The reason why the A.M.A. persisted in their campaign stemmed from an unfortunate episode which took place in the early stages of Abrams' experiments with blood sample diagnosis. Intent on proving him a charlatan, someone cunningly substituted rabbit's blood for the human sample during a test of the Doctor's claims. When Abrams was unable to detect the substitution, his entire work was discredited in orthodox eyes. What the A.M.A. never understood, and what similar orthodox bodies of our own time cannot seem to grasp, is that the factor of Belief plays a major part in originating the phenomena. The power of disbelief (Doubt) can effectively nullify belief, thus destroying any creative scheme brought about by positive thinking.

Despite the negative influence of the A.M.A. the work of Abrams was not discarded, radionic research being taken up and furthered by enthusiasts on both sides of the Atlantic.

The next important sequence in its development took place during the early '40s when an English civil engineer, George de la Warr, produced a radionics machine of his own design. Covered in black leather, it was soon known as the 'black box'. One of the experiments which de la Warr and his wife undertook culminated in the ability to affect the growth of diseased plants by focussing 'radionic' energy at them through a lens system. As the work progressed, the de la Warrs found that not only could they irradiate plants by beaming energy directly at them, but also by focussing the machine on a photograph of the diseased plants. Next they conceived the notion that it might be possible to affect the soil itself by beaming at it energies or radiations that were the equivalent of plant nutrients. In a definitive experiment, they cleared two garden sites some eighty feet apart and allowed the soil to settle for a week. Then they photographed one of the sites and began a four week period of treatment using the photograph in their machine. The other site was left untreated. At the end of the period of irradiation, they planted cabbages in both plots and sat back to await developments. Two months later, the plants growing in the irradiated section were three times larger than those left to grow in the normal manner. Under the firm impression that the cause was due to the treated soil, notwithstanding the apparently bizarre method by which the 'treatment' was effected, the de la Warrs continued to experiment successfully, and it was not long before they were approached by a nationally known firm of plant breeders who wished to acquire some treated soil in order to conduct an experiment of their own. De la Warr obliged, but the rigid test conditions imposed by the company's technicians gave negative results.

It was at this point that de la Warr began to suspect that their plants had been responding not to the treated soil, but to emanations from the humans involved in the tests. To prove this theory, de la Warr duplicated the experiments set by the company technicians on exactly the same plot of ground. To the bafflement of the laboratory staff, abnormally large growth was obtained. Again the technicians tried, but failed to achieve the results enjoyed by de la Warr.

Face to face with a devastating new truth, de la Warr set out to verify the reality of the human factor, and to do so conclusively, he set up several pots in which oat seedlings had been planted. The assistants concerning in watering the seedlings daily and monitoring their growth were told that particular pots contained irradiated soil, whilst the rest were not. In truth, none of the pots contained treated soil, the oat seedlings receiving only such nutrients provided by a normal, unadulterated soil. Yet, as the experiment progressed, those in the pots which the assistants *believed* to hold the treated soil actually grew faster and bigger than the others. Human belief, therefore, appeared to be affecting the cellular structure of the plants. Later, de la Warr wrote a book called *Mind Over Matter*, in which he declared that the real key to fostering healthy plants was to ask them to grow well. In a fifteen step procedure, the reader was asked to hold the seeds in his hand and invoke a blessing according to individual faith, and in a reverent and purposeful manner. In other words, de la Warr was advising his readers to employ the power of positive thinking. But the wording of his advice was enough to bring an immediate protest from the Catholic Church, who deemed it inadmissible for anyone below the rank of Deacon to perform the act of blessing. Notwithstanding this adjunct from on high, many readers followed de la Warr's instructions and reported success.

Another civil engineer, an American named Curtis P. Upton, whose father had been a partner of Thomas Edison, continued this line of research during the early '50s, turning his attention in particular to pest control. Following a theory of his own, he took an aerial photograph of a field of cotton which was plagued with an insect that destroyed the crop. The photograph was placed on a 'collector plate' in Upton's device, together with a reagent known to be poisonous to the cotton pests. The theory held was that the molecular structure of the emulsion on the photograph would be resonated at the identical frequency of the subject it represented pictorially. Thus, by affecting the photograph with a reagent known to be deadly to the cotton pests, Upton believed that the cotton plants in the field could be immunized against the insects – and because the amount of reagent used was infinitesimal compared to the size of acreage photographed, it was thought that conditions similar to the homoeopathic principle would be invoked. This bizarre treatment was completely successful and a million dollar crop was saved.

The next fascinating step in the evolution of Radionics was undertaken by a young engineer with the Kansas City Power and Light Company, T. Galen Hieronymus. Galen, an avid radio enthusiast before World War II, was approached one day by an elderly neighbour, a Dr Planck, with a request to machine some rather odd looking electrical parts. Beyond mentioning that he had studied new techniques with a medical genius in San Francisco, Planck gave no indication as to the purpose of the machine he was attempting to construct. There the matter seemed to rest, but on Planck's death some time later, the widow contacted Hieronymus, asking him to come to the house to sort through some strange machinery for which she had no use, saying that he could take away anything that he thought would be worthwhile. It was only then that Hieronymus discovered Planck's 'medical genius' to have been Dr Abrams.

Becoming interested, Hieronymus eventually built a Radionics box of his own – not for detecting energies emitted from diseased tissue, or from plants, but from metals, and with which he made discoveries that have not been fully evaluated to this day.

Some public interest in the story of Galen's research was aroused in the early '50s, when John Campbell, editor of *Astounding Science Fiction* magazine, printed a circuit diagram of the 'Hieronymus Machine'. Campbell had become interested in the 'impossible' device which, it was claimed, could analyse the component elements of an ore sample without the aid of spectroscopic, chemical, or other orthodox methods, and could influence – and even kill – living organisms, even from vast distances, with no scientifically understandable mechanism at the other end. Obtaining patents, Campbell constructed his own 'psionic' machine and experimented until at last he was sure that it did indeed do everything that had been claimed. One of the most significant interludes occurred during a visit to Hieronymus, when he asked the inventor if paper would conduct the invisible radionic energy by which the device operated. When Hieronymus said it wouldn't, Campbell drew out the circuit diagram of the machine, using India ink, which was a conductor. To the utter amazement of both men, the circuit diagram functioned just as well as the machine itself. Neither knew why, and in an interview held some twenty years later,

Hieronymus maintained that he still did not know.

The darker side of the machine's potential, a parallel of Upton's work, is reflected in two experiments performed by Hieronymus. Approached by farmers who were being troubled by worms which ate their corn crop, he took some newly-formed ears of the corn, twelve of which had worms inside. Choosing six in which the worms were of nearly identical size, he searched for and found a reagent that would reduce the vitality of the worms until they died. He then placed the infected ears in the machine which, in a short time, reduced the worms to white, damp spots.

On the second occasion, Hieronymus was asked if he could do anything about a plague of caterpillars, found on a friend's cherry tree each spring. Hieronymus instructed his friend to take a photograph of the tree, then to collect some of the caterpillars, along with a few freshly picked leaves, and send them all to him.

First, Hieronymus analysed the caterpillars to find the right reagent. 'We painted the photograph' he related, 'with the reagent – oil of cedar, I think it was – put the photo on the sensor plate, set the dials and just forgot about it.'

Three days later, when his friend turned into his driveway after returning from work, he was astonished to find his children stamping on caterpillars which were swarming in all directions away from the tree. A carpet of dead caterpillars lay directly under the tree, and more were falling off as he watched.

Hieronymus has remained close-mouthed about the exact method he applied to induce such an effect, although the knowledge is not his alone. The subject was broached in a letter to him from the bacteriologist Otto Rahn, who after studying the former's technique, wrote:

> Since those radiations hold the secret of life, they also hold the secret of death. At present, very few people know about the possibilities, and very few know all the facts. It seems imperative that those few keep their knowledge to themselves, and divulge only as much as is necessary to perform the immediate applications to cure disease. Your discoveries open up great possibilities, as

tremendous as those of the atom bomb, and just like atomic energy, these radiations may be used for the bad as well as for the good of humanity.

The crucial, tell-tale factor in the saga is Campbell's discovery that the circuit diagram alone of the Hieronymus machine worked just as well as the machine itself. 'Your electronic circuit,' he wrote to Hieronymus later, 'represents a pattern of relationships. The electrical characteristics are unimportant and can be dropped out completely.'

Campbell's conclusion was that the human mind itself is the instrument whereby detection of atomic emanations may be achieved. If he knew that the power of belief was the fundamental energy responsible for the phenomena, he was careful not to say so.

Another important factor for the present reader to consider is that all the instances recorded in this chapter showed a manifestation of the power only after a long period of concentration on the subject by the various experimenters. Is it not apparent, in the case of Campbell's discovery regarding the circuit diagram, that the strength of his *Belief* alone, having been well established by research into and construction of his 'psionic' machine, continued to function with the machine's symbol, the circuit diagram, bizarre though that may seem? Is it surprising that a newcomer to the science of Radionics, having been informed of such an astounding discovery, yet not having spent the appropriate period of concentration in which his belief can grow, fails to command the same power of manifestation?

Not every initiate gains inlet to the power by way of a sudden revelation, as in the experience of Bucke – and in any case, Bucke's command of the power was in the sphere of wisdom alone, not the apparently useless acquisition of the ability to bend metal, as with Geller. Eliphas Levi, as an initiate, penned a revealing sentence in *Transcendental Magic*, when he pointed out that

> Man can . . . project either active or passive light at Will; but he must acquire the consciousness of his power by dwelling habitually thereon. . . .

Chapter Five

It must by now be clear that the power of Belief is a fundamental, motivating force behind all human existence. Whatever activities we engage in, we do so because we believe we have the will to do them. Beliefs, in the form of the emotions like, dislike, fear, love, happiness, misery and the rest, rule over every second of our time. There is even a belief for most that we have no control over this process.

Emile Coué has shown that the power of Belief can heal the human body, and if we care to advance this line of thought, what is it but Belief which shapes the human body in the first place? A quaint observation regarding this concept appears in Austin Spare's *Book Of Pleasure*:

> A bat first grew wings . . . by its desire being organic enough to reach the subconscious. If its desire to fly had been conscious, it would have had to wait until it could have done so by the same means as ourselves, i.e. machinery.

The concept returns us to the age old query, only vaguely answered by Darwin's theory of natural selection; why has the giraffe such a long neck? The question may be expanded to ask why all the various forms of animals and insects emerge in their particular, strange and sometimes incomprehensible shapes?

To find an answer to this perplexing question we are obliged to return to the concept of an all-powerful Force which answers the call of every animate being's conscious belief, be it small or large. The Force, our Matrix, may be compared with a machine press which can mould matter like plastic material into any shape or form. The ideas and desires of each animate conscious mind, depending upon its level of intelligence, will determine the shape into which the body matter will eventually emerge during the course of evolution. Thus the giraffe now has a long neck because it believes that the leaves on certain trees are beneficial (it *likes* them, therefore it *desires* them). During its evolution, it did not wish to be as cumbersome as an elephant, so the body, having evolved to something not much larger than a horse and with which it was perfectly satisfied, remained a fixture. But it needed to reach the leaves on high branches of the trees, so the subconscious Force altered the animal's genes so as to extend the neck, in this way answering the giraffe's desire for its chosen fodder. This alteration of the genes, taking place at an atomic level, was carried out in response to the animal's *belief* that it could always reach the leaves. It was not something achieved consciously by the giraffe.

Man, with somewhat more intelligence and wholly different beliefs and desires, has evolved to a point where he or she feels the body to be perfectly balanced against the environment lived in, according to collective needs. Again, this has not been achieved by conscious will, but by the power of inner belief.

To refute this is to deny plain facts which are available to any interested researcher. To demonstrate how the Matrix, or subconscious Force, can adapt the human body, if called upon to do so, no more apt example presents itself than that of the Frenchman who calls himself *Monsieur Mangetout* (Mr Eat-It-All). Michel Lotito was born in Grenoble on June 15th 1950. At the age of nine years he began to eat glass and metal. Since 1966, his unusual gastronomic fare has included ten bicycles, a whole supermarket trolley in four and a half days, seven TV sets, six chandeliers, and a whole coffin, complete with handles. His most outstanding feat was performed in Caracas, Venezuela, where piece by piece, he gradually devoured a complete Cessna light aircraft.

Gastroenterologists who have X-rayed his abdominal tract have discovered that the intestines are twice as thick as in a normal person. It was also found that he has grown a double row of teeth which allows him to cope with his 'diet' of 2lb of metal a day. The abnormalities were certainly not present in childhood. What caused them to manifest? It appears that Lotito was born small, and thereafter, perhaps because of his diminutive size as a child, suffered stress through persecution by school bullies. It was during this period that he discovered that he could control pain mentally. Here, then, is a classic case of powerful positive thought. Whatever his reasons may have been, Lotito *believed* he could ingest abnormal materials, possibly to 'prove' himself, and his subconscious acted upon the strength of his belief, readjusting the internal body in order to cope with it.

I have described the eating of plates, metal and glass as abnormal, but in truth, abnormality is, up to a point, something which is determined by individual belief. Man's stomach is a factory designed to break down substances, its functions being adapted to deal with that which we currently believe to be natural fodder – that which is selected by means of our 'likes' and 'dislikes'. But it is really only our inherent belief that decided exactly what constitutes 'natural fodder'. The Aborigines will thrive on a diet of certain maggots, a delicacy to them but wholly repellent to a European. Equally, the Asians consume ants and grasshoppers with relish, simply because they 'like' (believe) them. Only our sense of taste, which is primarily there to warn us away from really dangerous materials, differentiates between cultural likes and dislikes.

Examples of instantaneous manifestation of the subconscious Force are even more of a strain on the understanding, even when the event is recorded by a reliable and intelligent body of witnesses. Yet the same key need only be applied to bring about complete de-mystification. The phenomenon of 'miracle' healing is an example of how the subconscious power acts to return the physical body to the shape and form originally dictated by its evolutionary gene pattern, into which it grew before some damage brought about deformity. The first name to spring to mind in this respect will undoubtedly be Lourdes, the shrine in southern France, near the Spanish-French border in the Pyrenees. Of the healing phenomena which have taken place there, I shall select two, and I make no apologies for choosing the most extreme of cases.

First, the story of Pierre de Rudder, a Belgian workman who suffered a crushed left leg when involved in an accident with a falling tree. His shin bone was broken in two places, with a small piece of it eventually breaking away to lodge itself in the surrounding tissue. When the piece was removed by surgery, it left an open wound which refused to heal. The remaining lengths of shinbone were therefore separated by a space of three centimetres.

In excruciating pain, Rudder sought the advice of several medical experts, all of whom declared that nothing could be done except amputation. But Rudder steadfastly refused to permit his leg to be taken off, despite the agony of his plight. His leg was perpetually bandaged and he could hardly move, even with the aid of crutches. Its lower part could be moved in all directions and the heel lifted in such a way as to fold the leg in the middle of the shin. The foot could be twisted until it was completely reversed, its movement only restricted by the soft tissue. Obviously, Rudder was unable to work and his family were forced to live on charity.

Eight years after the accident Rudder gave up all hope of a cure by orthodox means and, being a devout Catholic, made plans for a pilgrimage to the shrine at Lourdes. Before he set out, he was examined by a doctor, who confirmed the extent of his injuries, testifying that he could plainly see the two ends of the broken shinbone in the ever open wound. It was also stated that Rudder had a second wound on the top of his foot, with witnesses confirming that both were in a very poor condition.

In April 1875 Rudder dragged himself the mile and a half to the railway station with the aid of two crutches and helped by his wife, an initial effort which took him two hours. A railway employee carried him into the train, but when he saw how Rudder's leg was dangling helplessly, couldn't help commenting upon the wisdom of making the journey. The injured man replied that as others had been cured at Lourdes, so he might be, too.

After a horrendously painful journey, Rudder and his wife at last reached the little cave and grotto in which the statue of Our Lady had been erected. Rudder himself collapsed exhausted to the ground, but so crowded was it with pilgrims that his injured leg was repeatedly stumbled over, causing him intense agony. He tried to walk around the cave as the others were doing, but after only two circuits was forced to sit down once more. There he prayed, begging to be cured so that he might support his wife and child as in the past. Suddenly, as he later related, he was overwhelmed by a strange feeling. Deeply moved, and without thinking, he rose and walked through the crowds to kneel before the statue. And then he realised what he had done. In rapture, he began walking round the cave. For the first time since his accident, he was able to walk naturally. His wife, the shock of astonishment proving too much for her, fainted on the spot.

Rudder was taken to a nearby house where his leg was critically examined. Not only were both wounds now closed, but the shin bone was no longer broken. And most astounding of all was that both legs, notwithstanding the missing three centimetre piece, were now of equal length, as they had been prior to the accident.

This incident carries the sworn testimony of the doctors who examined Rudder, both before his pilgrimage and immediately after his triumphant return. But the most astounding aspect of the affair came to light more than twenty years later, after Rudder's death from pneumonia. In the interests of medical knowledge, permission was granted for an autopsy to take place. On May 24th, 1899 Dr Van Hoestenberghe amputated both legs at the knee so that the bones could be examined and photographed. It was found that although the deformity of the left leg was still visible, the healing had taken place in such a way that the two legs were of equal length. The three centimetre fragment of shin bone which had been removed by surgery had been replaced by a piece of healthy white bone of exactly the right shape and length, perfectly knitted into the separated strips of original bone.

The mystifying event of Rudder's cure was not regarded as a 'miracle' by the authorities until 1908, by which time the Lourdes Medical Bureau had been set up in order to verify all claims to recovery by faith alone. More than five thousand cures have been recorded to date by the Bureau. A number of these cases have been thoroughly investigated and a small proportion declared to be *medically inexplicable*. Of the cures which have been examined by the Church, only sixty four in the last hundred years have been recorded as 'miraculous'. One of these was 'Pierre de Rudder of Jabbeke, Belgium, who was miraculously cured of an ununited fracture of the left leg at the age of 52 on the 7th April 1875'.

The second instance, which took place in 1923 and was even more closely investigated by the Bureau, was that of an Irishman named John Traynor. At the age of 32 Traynor was wounded in the head during fighting at Antwerp, in October 1914. Unconscious for five weeks, he eventually recovered and was ultimately posted to Egypt, where he was promptly wounded again. After a second recovery, he volunteered for the Gallipoli landing in April 1915, in the process of which he became caught in a burst of machine gun fire. Apart from sustaining another wound to the head, two bullets passed through the right side of his chest, while another crossed the chest and upper right arm to lodge under his right collarbone, cutting the brachial plexus, the nerves of the shoulder and the upper arm. Consequently, his right arm was completely paralysed.

Having been shipped back to his home in Liverpool, four more operations were carried out in an effort to suture the nerves, but all were unsuccessful, and to compound matters, Traynor soon began to suffer with epilepsy. The surgeons finally urged him to have his paralysed right arm amputated, but the Irishman stubbornly refused and went home to eke out a precarious existence on the War Pension that had been awarded him.

In a short time, however, his epilepsy became worse, he became incontinent and both legs suffered partial paralysis. In April 1920 his skull was trepanned and a silver plate inserted to protect his brain, after which, his condition continuing to deteriorate, he soon became confined to a wheel chair, being lifted in and out of bed each day. For three years he remained at his home, existing in conditions of extreme poverty and pain, until July 1923, when he was admitted to the Mosely Hill Home for Incurables. Just at that time, however, Traynor had found out that the diocesan pilgrimage to Lourdes began its journey from Liverpool, and became obsessed with the idea of joining it. Using his last reserves of cash as a down payment, he persuaded his wife to pawn everything they had in order to raise the rest. In vain the priests in charge of the pilgrimage tried to dissuade him from attempting the journey, being of the opinion that he was in so bad a condition that he was liable to die before ever reaching the shrine. Even his doctor refused to issue a certificate of fitness for the journey.

During the long train ride across France, his condition worsened alarmingly, and at three stops enquiries were made regarding the proximity of local hospitals so that he could be put off the train, apparently in a state close to death. But each time, there was found to be no hospital nearby.

At his arrival at the Asile Hospital in Lourdes, Traynor suffered a major epileptic fit, during which he started to bleed at the mouth. Three pilgrimage doctors who examined him at this time confirmed all his afflictions and condition in a jointly signed statement.

Two days later, on the afternoon of July 26th, Traynor was wheeled down and immersed in the baths. For a few moments, all went well, but then he suddenly began to thrash his legs around. The startled attendants assumed he was undergoing yet another epileptic fit and when Traynor started to get to his feet, feeling that he could easily do so, they held him down. When he was lifted from the bath, he felt so weak and tired that he burst into tears. Still restrained, he was then taken to join the procession of the Blessed Sacrament, where all the sick are assembled every afternoon in front of the basilicas. As the Archbishop of Rheims passed in front of him, carrying the monstrance, Traynor realised that, for the first time since the battle of Gallipoli, eight years previously, he could move his right arm. And move it he did – so vigorously that it tore loose from its fastenings. At the same time, he tried to rise from his stretcher, but again the attendants held him down, and under the impression that he had become hysterical, administered a sedative injection. On his return to Asile Hospital, however, doctors noted and recorded the fact that Traynor could 'walk seven steps, although with great difficulty', and that his reflexes were restored. They prescribed more sedation and attendants were instructed to watch him while he slept.

Early next morning, Traynor awoke and then climbed unaided out of his bed to dash from the ward, pushing aside anyone who got in his way. In his bare feet and pursued by two attendants, he ran the several hundred yards of gravel path from the hospital to the Grotto, where he remained in prayer for twenty minutes, oblivious of the crowd that gathered about him. Then he returned to the ward where he washed and dressed. Throughout this time, he was mentally confused, apparently aware that he had experienced an extraordinary recovery, but with no clear recollection of his previous condition. Consequently, he was at first mystified and then slightly irritated at the constant inquiries after his health.

The Liverpool pilgrimage was due to make its return journey on the following day, but before being allowed to leave with them, Traynor was examined once more by the doctors. They found that having recovered the sensation in his legs, his gait was now normal; there had been no recurrence of the epileptic attacks since the cure, and he could use his right arm. Most astounding of all, the hole in his skull was considerably smaller.

Only during the train journey back through France did Traynor seem to realise the full extent of his metamorphosis. And it appeared the cure was still having its effects, for subsequent examination disclosed that both his epilepsy and paralysis were gone. Except for a minor deformity of the muscles in his hand, his right arm was fully restored to normal – and where there had formerly been a hole in his skull, there was now only a slight depression.

Later, as a fully active man once more, John Traynor went into the haulage business and was capable of lifting sacks of coal weighing 200 lbs.

Four years after the event, the Lourdes Medical Bureau declared that his cure could not have been accomplished by any normal means

> . . . because of the certain knowledge of the pre-existing lesions which had not responded to surgical treatment, because of the suddeness of the cure and lack of convalescence, and because the cure persisted.

I repeat that cases like those of Rudder and Traynor are extremely rare, although there are a number of others, fully documented, in which the cure was instantaneous – one of lupus of the face, a form of tuberculosis known as 'dog's muzzle', and another from a seriously advanced condition of tuberculosis peritonitis. The latter cure was dramatic enough to witness. In what appeared to be the final stages of the disease, the patient spitting blood, a pulse rate of 150 and face turning blue, immersion into the baths resulted in a sudden and complete recovery in front of a number of witnesses, one of whom was a doctor.

All these are extreme instances of *involuntary* positive thinking, their dramatic but unchallengeable results being an assault on the logic of the so-called rational mind, and yet giving justification to the older, religious manuscripts which seem to over-glorify the 'Power of the Lord', and to the tracts of the Alchemists in which such glowing and reverent terms are employed to describe the beneficial effects of the Philosophers' Stone.

It may be argued that manifestations of this great power, in this instance working for the good of mankind, vindicates the religious ideals of the Church fundamentalists who believe implicitly in the physical existence of Jesus and his mother, Mary, and their high sanctification after death, for the shrine at Lourdes is a cult of the Immaculate Conception, authorized by the Church as such since 1862. Unprejudiced examination of the necessary historical data, however, will show that the peasant girl, Bernardette, whose vision drew nationwide attention to the spot in 1858, did not see the Virgin Mary, as the Church would wish everyone to believe – and that the Church ultimately authorized the cult in the name of the Immaculate Conception with some reluctance, only finally doing so in order to prevent the belief of the peasantry from focussing on superstition rather than on the established tenets of the Church itself.

The success of the cures is not due merely to the sanctification of the place as a shrine of Our Lady, Mother of Christ, Mary of the Immaculate Conception, but rather because the pilgrims concerned *believed that a cure would take place*. Had historical circumstances been different and a heritage of authenticity been attached to the story of Jack and the Beanstalk instead of to the Testament stories, sick people could have made their pilgrimage to the Holy Shrine of Our Jack of the Immaculate Horticultural Manifestation, and had exactly the same chance of being cured miraculously. A successful cure depends upon the pilgrim adopting the right attitude of mind which will allow the notion of a cure to transfer from the conscious mind to the subconscious. Admittedly, fundamentalist awe of Our Lady will play a great part in focussing the power of belief, but manifestation of the power does nothing to justify the idea that religious doctrine alone is responsible. In fact, religious belief can work to the detriment of the pilgrim, as well as to the good, the results in some cases being horrific.

In January 1881, an anonymous healer quoted an alchemical maxim when he wrote:

> There is nothing but Mind; we are expressions of the One Mind; the body is only a mortal belief; *as man thinketh so is he*.

The gist of the last sentence has been repeated by knowledgeable writers from early times right up to the present day, in various ways according to individual approach. In 1960, the cosmetic surgeon Maxwell Maltz, used these words to convey the ancient truth:

> The Creative Mechanism within you is impersonal. It will work automatically and impersonally to achieve goals of success and happiness, or of unhappiness and failure, depending upon the goals which you yourself set for it.

Ralph Waldo Emerson, the American philosopher, echoed the same sentiment, but in a way that sounded a note of warning:

> Beware of what you want for you will get it.

To be sure, he was assuming that if subconscious power is brought into play, its effects would take place over a period of time. But the same maxim applies to instantaneous manifestations – and never was a truth more devastatingly realised than in the phenomenon of stigmata as experienced by the unfortunate St Francis of Assisi.

Stigmata – the appearance in the flesh of the wounds supposed to have been inflicted on Christ during his crucifixion – was once the object of supreme scorn and scepticism, but nowadays, setting aside the few known cases of self-inflicted wounds, the reality of the phenomenon is fully recognised. It has taken place in too many instances under close medical scrutiny to be doubted, the event recorded not merely by competent witnesses alone, but also by cameras. The only question that has not been resolved is its cause. Academics have come close to the answer when they postulated a condition of psycho-neurosis (hysteria) as the factor responsible for its manifestation, and certainly there is evidence that the key lies within the individual's own mind. Not long ago, an American girl in whom the stigmata appeared was relieved of the symptoms by hypnosis, while in 1933, a Lutherian doctor in Germany succeeded in producing stigmata in a hysterical patient by use of similar hypnotic suggestion. The religious idea that the wounds are inflicted by an invisible, external deity, imported as a living reminder of the suffering which Christ endured for mankind, is losing the credibility that it once widely enjoyed – and rightly so. The historical records of the stigmatization of St Francis (Francesco) of Assisi in 1224 contain all the clues necessary to arrive at a correct deduction of the cause, and perhaps it is best to begin by reminding the reader that the subject was a fundamentalist to the point of obsession. After turning from a life of pleasure to one of sacrifice and service to the poor and diseased, he founded the Franciscan Order of monks, the members of which were pledged to absolute poverty. Even their original dress, a coarse, grey habit with a pointed hood, epitomised poverty, humility and self-abasement.

At the time of the phenomenon, Francis was observing the literal word of the Testaments, having ascended the mount to spend forty days in a cave where he prayed. In the words of the monks themselves, he was 'keeping a lent in honour of the Blessed Virgin Mary, Mother of God, and Blessed Michael, the Archangel, from the feast of the assumption of St Mary the Virgin to the feast of St Michael in September.' It was while in deep, meditational prayer, outside his cave one day, that Francis experienced an hallucination of a 'seraph', an angel which bore the marks of the crucifixion. The shock was such that he fell into a faint. According to eye-witnesses, it was as he recovered from the swoon and attempted to get to his feet, calling for help as he did so, that the stigmata appeared.

Thomas of Celano, in an account written in 1229, three years after the death of Francis, records this account of the unique wounds:

> His hands and feet seemed pierced in the midst by nails, the heads of the nails appearing in the inner part of the hands and in the upper part of the feet and their points were over against them. . . .

Note that Celano is describing not just wounds such as a nail might make, but the formation of hardened tissue in the shape of nails and lodged in the wound. Other accounts maintain that the 'nails' in his feet protruded so much that he was unable to walk. Further, there was a scar in his right side, as if the body had at some time been pierced by a lance, and which often trickled blood. Corroboration of the presence of sinewy nails is to be found in the *Book of Miracles (Tractatus de Miraculis)*, written between 1274 and 1275:

> . . . they saw in the hands and feet not the fissures of the nails but the nails themselves marvellously wrought by the power of God, indeed implanted in the flesh itself, in such wise that if they were pressed in one either side they straightway, as if they were one piece of sinew, projected on the other. They also saw his side reddened with blood. We who recount these things ourselves witnessed them, we felt them with the same hands with which we now write. . . .

According to the *Testimony of Brother Leo*, one of the earliest references to the stigmata, Francis afterwards wrote out some praises:

> . . . giving thanks to God for the favour which had been conferred on him.

Here, then, is an instance of a deeply implanted fundamentalist belief being successfully transferred to the subconscious whilst the conscious mind was in a state of trance, or what medical men of today would term 'hysteria' (psychoneurosis). In the cases of Rudder and Traynor at Lourdes, a similar state of mind was momentarily attained, no doubt in response to the heightened tension of the occasion coupled with the intense pain which both men were enduring, allowing a transfer to the subconscious of a belief that a cure would be effected. With Francis, the belief was that he would, after sufficient humbleness, poverty and prayer, be as Christ was in his finest hour, so to speak – and the subconscious, impregnated with the idea, duly obliged. Unluckily for Francis – however much of a 'favour' he thought it to be – the transition was one of the instantaneous kind.

It is only natural for the fundamentalist to argue against this interpretation, but evaluation of all aspects must be logically considered, without the prejudice of an ingrained belief. If, as the fundamentalists would have everyone believe, the Crucifixion took place in reality and the description of the wounds in the Gospel is accurate, then it would not be unreasonable to expect that an external spiritual power that is connected with the event and is responsible for inflicting the phenomenon, would be bound to duplicate the exact type of wounds at each manifestation. But this is not the case, and in truth, the variety of phenomena which comes under the blanket term 'stigmata' is worth a study in itself. Some recipients, like St Catharine of Ricci, or St Gemma Calgani, although temporally some four hundred years apart, exhibit the additional stigmata of deformed shoulders, both complaining of the pain and great weight of an invisible cross. Nowhere in the Gospels, however, is there recorded the fact that Jesus suffered with deformed shoulders, and we all recall that Simon of Cyrene was compelled to carry the cross (Matt 27, 32). The deformity of the shoulders, therefore, is an embellishment of the story added by the victim's own imagination and made 'real' by the active power of belief.

The most powerful argument against the fundamentalist point of view is presented by such alternative stigmata, including Luminosity, or Espousal. The latter is a phenomenon parallel to that of stigmata, but where certain virgins dedicated to a holy life suffer the spontaneous manifestation of a 'ring' of flesh on their marriage finger – an 'espousal' with Christ and an obvious figment of an overactive imagination. A typical case, occurring in France, 1874, is described in *La Stigmatization*, by its author, Dr Imbert-Gourbeyre, who received evidence from eye-witnesses.

It is a vivid red line encircling the finger, with tiny crosses occurring at intervals. The bezel represents a heart pierced with three swords. This ring shows much more conspicuously on Sundays, when it shines with extraordinary brilliance. It is not formed of little clots of blood adhering to the skin, but it is just a red mark, probably accompanied by a thickening of the epidermis.

The subject in this instance was a twenty-five year old girl who, in the words of a local physician:

. . . is a simple child whose mind is fixed upon the Host and the ciborium.

Luminosity is a phenomenon where, while in a state of ecstasy, or shallow trance, the subject's chemical make up is radically altered, signified externally by an increased rate of breathing, a high pulse rate and the production of phosphorescent chemicals in the skin or blood. In 1934, the phenomenon was filmed and a report submitted to a medical society connected with the University of Padua, in Italy. Dr Protti, who investigated the event and wrote the report, made it quite clear that the subject in question, a woman

. . . had a fixed idea of a religious character.

Such a manifestation may be at first deemed impossible, especially the necessary chemical change in the body, but exactly the same chemical reaction is observed on a summer's night when a glow-worm attempts to attract a mate, while in the ocean, the phosphorescent fish does likewise. In human subjects, the cause is due to religious mania, in particular the belief that when associated with Christ, or Heaven, there will be a 'radiance', or a 'splendour of light' as described in the Scriptures and other religious texts. Achieving the same disassociation of the conscious mind, the subject's subconscious reacts to the implanted idea of 'illumination'. In stark reality, away from the erroneous imaginative interpretations of the religious crank, the 'illumination' therein referred to is the illumination of the mind, the development of the understanding. When the trance, or ecstasy wears off, and the conscious mind reasserts itself, the body chemistry returns to normal and the phenomenon disappears.

Another religious ideal, highly esteemed by devout believers in the literal word of the Bible, is that of Eternal Life, or Immortality – and this, too, the subconscious power has endeavoured to bestow upon those who have asked for it, although in a macabre manner which the recipients could hardly have forseen. I refer, as you may have guessed, to the Incorruptibles, the corpses of 'saintly' persons, generally women, which defy the natural process of decomposition. I exclude those which are due to natural elements, such as the perfectly preserved head of a Tollund man, dating from the Iron Age. After being killed by strangulation, the victim was thrown into a bog, the chemical compound of which served to preserve the head and face to an amazing degree. Similar finds have been made in the peat bogs of Scotland and Ireland, but such bodies are not incorrupt by deliberate intent of the subjects themselves. Neither are those preserved by mummification, or by being immersed in a special preservative, or by the curious natural process known as soapification, in which the body tissues are gradually reduced to an ammoniacal soap beneath a toughened outer skin. This results from burial in a damp soil in the proximity of existing putrification, although there is a random element in its manifestation which baffles the experts. The religious phenomenon known as the Holy Incorruptibles, is an entirely different matter, for the lack of decay cannot be explained away in rational terms. One example is that of the body of St Teresa Margaret, who died in 1770. Today, it can be seen in a glass coffin in Florence, showing no signs of putrification, although there is some slight discolouration. How remarkable this is may be judged by those who recall that St Teresa died of gangrene, her corpse rigid, swollen and purple just after death. Two days later, it had assumed a near normal appearance and has stayed that way ever since.

Astonishingly, it has been found that the corpses of Holy Incorruptibles will not decay even when interred in conditions that would hasten the normal process of decomposition, some remaining intact even though buried in ground so damp that the interment clothes have completely rotted away.

Like stigmata, Incorruptibility is not automatically bestowed upon the holy and virtuous, for there are a great many Christian saints who did not receive this 'divine favour'. On the other hand, some of those who did were never beatified or cannonized, a state of affairs which has perplexed and embarrassed Church authorities.

This phenomenon has the same principle at its foundation as that of stigmata: the power of the subject's devout belief – in this case, in everlasting life. In the trauma of approaching death, their minds generate the required conditions for the subconscious to respond. Unfortunately, the ignorance of the subject, whose desire is conceived in terms of *human existence only*, ensures that it is the physical body which is granted everlasting life in the only way possible after the animating spirit has left it. Hence the rejection of decay. If this appears to be an unwarranted judgement on those who hold a vision of immortality, pause for rationalisation will reveal that to think in terms of earthly existence when attempting to imagine life after physical death is a common failing. Spiritualists have fallen into this trap for decades, their active imaginations envisaging a happy land, far away, to which departed souls travel, there to pursue only the most agreeable activities of the human experience. As for the mechanical mystery of how decomposition is held in check, it must be remembered that all matter is, as Einstein pointed out, nothing but congealed electricity – even 'dead' bodies. In the instance of this particular phenomenon, the electrical atoms of the corpse have been altered by the power of Belief.

The most intriguing aspect of the Incorruptibles is the knowledge – once the cause is realised and accepted – that the power can operate successfully on inanimate objects like corpses, as well as animated bodies. We only perceive a corpse to be inanimate because its driving force, the personality, has left it. But the atomic structure of the matter which constitutes the corpse is still full of movement in its role as 'congealed electricity'. In the normal course of events, that atomic structure would be programmed into a movement which incorporates a radical redistribution of itself from the form which it has held, because the force field which dictated that form, the matrix, has been removed. In the case of an Incorruptible, however, the force field is retained, the power of the subject's belief having instituted a different programming.

This avenue of reasoning may go some way towards the explanation of mysteries such as a plaster statue of Christ that can shed real blood, or a painting of the Virgin that can cry real tears. The former is a figure owned by Mrs Anne Poore, of Pennsylvania, USA. Just after Easter 1975 she was kneeling in front of the 26-inch high plaster image, praying for all those souls who had turned away from the Church. Looking up suddenly, she was startled to see drops of blood appear in the carved wounds on the palms of the statue. Subsequently, the blood flowed on several occasions, but by that time, Mrs Poore had made the statue into a shrine on her porch where a great many more people were able to witness the marvel. On Fridays and holy days, the flow of blood was particularly copious.

Eventually, the image was moved into the Episcopalian Church of St Luke's, at Eddystone, where it was mounted on a platform above the altar. Given this opportunity to examine the phenomenon at length, the church pastor has reported that the bleeding has sometimes lasted as long as four hours. Another priest, arriving as a sceptic, went away convinced that he had witnessed a miracle. He said

> 'I have personally taken the hands off the statue – they are held in place by wooden dowels – and examined them. They are solid chalk. And the statue bled profusely as I watched. . . .'

To de-mystify this phenomenon we have only to note that Mrs Poore is a woman with the most devout religious convictions, and therefore it is her subconscious power which has activated the blood flow – at an atomic level. Her devotion to the image, carried out just after Easter worship, would naturally focus on the Crucifixion theme, and although it may seem blasphemous to the pious, I can only remark that it is a pity that her power, like that of Uri Geller, has manifested in such a trivial manner. To heal the sick, for example, would have been much more worthwhile.

Readers may doubt the interpretation above on the grounds that Mrs Poore is not reported to have been in a state of psycho-neurosis, or to have fallen in a swoon, or trance, at the time the bleeding first manifested. Engaged in deep prayer she may have been, but apparently quite oblivious to the fact that her subconscious had begun to produce the phenomenon. In reply, I can only refer you to the case of Steve Hoholik, who had no idea his 'message' was being broadcast, or perhaps to the many cases of poltergeist activity, where inanimate objects are levitated and thrown about the room. It is nowadays unanimously agreed to be the product of an emotionally stressed mind, its owner entirely unaware of being the cause. The only difference between the two is that, with Mrs Poore, religious belief is instigating the activity.

Any violent or traumatic situation, in which established beliefs are invoked with sufficient intensity, may set in motion a pattern of phenomena – much as the battle of Delville Woods in France, during the First World War. It was a bitter and bloody action in which more than 2,000 soldiers lost their lives.

After the engagement, surviving members of the South African Pioneer Corps made a memorial cross from a length of pine cut from Delville Woods. It was taken back to South Africa to be erected where it stands today, in the Garden of Remembrance at Pietermaritzburg, near Durban. Every July since 1919, resin oozes like tears from the knots in the wood, commencing a few days prior to the anniversary of the battle, and stopping a day or so afterwards.

In normal circumstances, resin will ooze from a cut pine for about eighteen months after the wood is dead. Botannical experts can find no reason why the wood of the Pietermaritz-burg Cross, now dead for seventy years, should continue to ooze resin, or why it does so once a year at the same time every year.

Our individual philosophical convictions, religious or otherwise, are the motivating forces which dictate what form a manifestation of phenomena might take, should the conditions be right for it to do so. In the sphere of religious belief, it has been noted as a statistic that stigmatics are almost exclusively members of the Catholic Church, showing that its indoctrination was deep indeed. The most extreme case of stigmata ever recorded, and one which exemplifies the tremendous power of belief, is that of Teresa Neumann, whose history is fully documented in a biography written by Johannes Steiner, published in 1967. Teresa, born in Bavaria in 1898 and of a poor background, was engaged in menial work until overcome by a mysterious illness which incapacitated her. But in 1926, all her ills were instantaneously cured after she experienced a vision that left her suffering with recurring stigmata. Over the following thirty two years each Friday saw her gushing blood from wounds in the hands and feet, sometimes losing as much as a pint, with an accompanying weight loss of eight pounds. Yet on the Sunday after each manifestation she appeared normal.

Taking full advantage of her periods of trance and unconsciousness, doctors examined her regularly and with great thoroughness, their reports frequently annotating the appearance of nail-like formations akin to those first seen in the case of St Francis of Assisi. An added facet of Teresa's case was her belief in the sustaining properties of the Communion wafer and wine, which was the sole food to pass her lips for the last thirty-five years of her life. Her excreta ceased after 1930 and her intestinal tract completely withered away. Yet she remained fairly active, experiencing ecstasies and visions until her death in 1962.

In the concluding pages of *The Physical Phenomena of Mysticism* (1952), author Herbert Thurston, having documented many instances of stigmata, brings attention to the fact that, prior to the story of St Francis of Assisi, not a single genuine case of stigmata was reported. No sooner, however, was the extraordinary circumstances of St Francis circulated throughout the world, than other irrefutable cases of the phenomenon began to occur among simple, unsophisticated and devout people, and have continued to occur without intermission ever since. Thurston rightly infers that St Francis created what he terms a 'crucifixion complex', a religious idea which entered the minds of many to become a pious obsession. As a comparison, and in an alternative sphere to that of religion, it may be suggested that older readers will recall that a similar sequence of events took place at the advent of the first flying saucer sighting.

The least acceptable statement made in *Hermes Unveiled* was the assertion that the image on the Shroud of Turin was put there by an advanced practitioner in the art of positive thinking, projecting his mental vision of Christ's figure by a mastered power of Belief. Perhaps, in the light of the various phenomena just discussed, such an idea will not appear quite so improbable.

All such phenomena are instituted at an atomic level and the concept of mind power impressing an image on a winding sheet is no more outlandish than rare cases of levitation, or of an object being lifted and thrown across the room by the mind of a disturbed child. Fundamentalists will cling to their conviction that the subject of the image, Christ's figure, is vindication enough for their belief in a real Jesus, although I have adequately shown the figure to be culled from Hermetic symbolism. If that is not enough, I point out that the Shroud itself, image apart, is part of a long established symbolic scheme. The original idea stemmed from early Egyptian Mystery rites, as part of a ritual known as the *rebirth*. It is not uncommon to find Old Kingdom carvings or sculptures of the god Osiris (personifying the subconscious) in the form of a mummy, enveloped in a funeral shroud as he lies awaiting *resurrection* (the development of the understanding). In extremely early rituals the form of Osiris is extended on, or wrapped in, an animal skin – that of a cow, the sacred Cow-goddess, Nut, who is the *mother* (reflection – the Hermetic process) of Osiris. This section of the Mysteries is known as the Animal Rebirth. There were, over the ages, several variations to the theme, the animal skin in one instance representing Set (the conscious mind). It was this cradle of skin through which Osiris had to pass before being *reborn as a child*.

Under the later Dynasties, the New Kingdom, the skin had been superceded by the more familiar shroud, which at first was speckled like a leopard skin, the Hermetic meaning of which I have already made clear in the expositions. In later times still, the speckling was dropped and a plain *white* shroud took its place – merely a development of an old established Hermetic symbol and still retaining the same hidden meaning.

Chapter Six

On September 8th 1980 banner headlines on two continents brought news of the death of ex-Beatle, John Lennon, after he had been shot down outside a New York hotel. As the star lay dying, his killer, Mark Chapman, stood quietly to one side awaiting the arrival of the police. Onlookers noticed that he was clutching a copy of J.D. Salinger's best selling novel, *Catcher In The Rye*. At his trial, Chapman offered no explanation for the killing, but when sentenced, astounded the court by reading aloud a short passage from the book. Subsequent interrogation revealed that the boy had become obsessed with the novel since first reading it at the age of sixteen, gradually identifying himself with its hero, Holden Caufield, portrayed by the author as a Pied Piper style of character who distrusted adults and carried on a personal crusade against their hypocrisy. Some months before the killing, Chapman had read a magazine article disclosing details about Lennon's private life and business activities, showing him to be more of a multi-million dollar executive than a figurehead of the 'pop' scene. Further material absorbed by Chapman proposed that the famous bed sit-in for peace by John and Yoko was really no more than a publicity stunt. Suddenly, Chapman had seen Lennon as part of the adult, hypocritical world rather than of the fantasy world of rock music. Disillusioned, he became determined to kill the star, and in his adopted role as 'Catcher in the Rye', stalked his quarry until an opportunity presented itself.

This obsession with the book, his sympathy with the philosophy expounded in it, appear to be damning evidence of the way in which fictional permissiveness – over-dramatised emotions, immorality and violence – purveyed to millions by way of literature and television, is a detrimental influence on receptive minds, despite the protestations of publishers and TV moguls whose interests lie in denying it.

The real reason why such influence takes effect in specific

cases can hardly be guessed, although it has been conceded that there exists a deeper thread of mystery running through the whole of the Chapman saga which cannot be identified by referral to established patterns of behaviour. It is certainly the case that Chapman was mentally receptive to *Catcher In The Rye* philosophy, although a definitive interpretation of its exact intent is hard to come by. Even the author, since the controversy, has refused to interpret it, saying that people must make up their own minds. The hero is portrayed throughout as overwhelmed with the futility of life and desperately seeks for some way in which to end it. So closely identified did Chapman become with the book's theme that he, too, looked for a way to escape, a quest which, at one point, drove him into an abortive attempt at suicide. With the failure of this attempt, and his subsequent appraisal of the material about John Lennon, he felt that he could relieve his torment by killing Lennon, thereby removing from the world a symbol of gross hypocrisy, and by being incarcerated for the crime, which was in some measure a method of removing himself from the futility of everyday life. But an air of the bizarre overshadowed the story when details of Chapman's movements during the period leading up to the crime were eventually released. In *Catcher In The Rye*, there is no murder, but the hero spends three days in New York, wandering in the vicinity of Central Park, indulging in odd behaviour, until at last discovering a merry-go-round. Chapman came to New York and literally acted out the same three day sequence in the identical area, but then went on to commit his crime. He maintained that he did not intentionally follow the routine described in the book, but once there, felt compelled to do so by an *inner impulse*.

One other astounding detail in the connection between Lennon, Chapman and *Catcher In The Rye* has been noticed. At the time just prior to his death, Lennon, after having been a virtual recluse for a number of years, had decided to become active in the music business once more and had recorded some new songs. The lyrics of one of them contain mention of a 'merry-go-round'. Investigators felt that this was something more than coincidence, although unable to explain it in any other way.

If literature is a possible danger to receptive but immature minds, the events which took place at Hungerford, in Berkshire, on the afternoon of August 19th 1987 seem similarly to indict the motion picture industry. Twenty seven year old Michael Ryan rampaged through the town, killing sixteen people before turning the gun on himself. Since that Wednesday afternoon, attention has been drawn to the marked resemblance between Ryan's orgy of violence and the scenario of the film *First Blood*. In the picture, the trail of death begins with a murder in a forest, followed by another at a petrol filling station, before the killer goes on to terrorise a small town community. Ryan, wearing a Rambo style headband and carrying arms and ammunition, murdered a woman in Savernake Forest, shot a petrol station attendant, and then strode through the streets of Hungerford firing indiscriminately.

Such real life mirroring of imaginary situations has been noticed before, generally in connection with literature rather than any other medium, investigation tending to reveal that its scope is so wide as to cast considerable doubt on the stock explanation that it is all coincidence.

In 1977, an American writer and musician, Herbert Greenhouse, authored a book entitled *Premonitions*, a work which reflected his alternative interest as an avid investigator of the paranormal. At the opening of chapter sixteen, which has as its title 'Creating the Future', Greenhouse asks of his readers the following questions:

> Did Jules Verne know more than a hundred years ago that *Apollo XI* would land on the moon in July 1969? Was he subliminally, if not consciously, getting 'feedback' from the future when in 1865 he wrote his novel *From The Earth To The Moon*, and in 1870, *Round The Moon*. Feedback from ideas that he himself may have projected into the next century and that set in motion a chain of events leading to the successful moon landing?

Greenhouse, wrote a book entitled *Premonitions*, a work similarity between Verne's imaginary moon-shot and the real thing – that Verne's spacecraft, named *Columbiad*, was cone-shaped in appearance, as was the *Apollo XI* command module, the *Columbia*. There were three astronauts in both imaginary and real spacecraft, and Verne's launching area was situated in Cape Town, Florida, not far from the present Cape Kennedy. Verne's flight calculation estimated that the *Columbiad* would reach the moon in 97 hours, 13 minutes and 20 seconds. In fact, *Columbia* averaged 97 hours and 39 minutes each way. Many more 'coincidences' between the imaginary data in the two Verne novels and the real space flight were annotated, including the fact that Verne, a Frenchman, had chosen to nominate America as the country from which his fictitious space exploration would emanate.

Earlier in his own book, Greenhouse had joined the many writers who have remarked upon the astounding similarities between Morgan Robertson's fictional liner, the *Titan*, and the ill-fated *Titanic* – the story by now a familiar theme.

In 1898 Morgan Robertson, an ex-sailor turned novelist, wrote *The Wreck Of The Titan*, a story in which a great ocean liner, bigger than any craft afloat at the time, was in collision with a giant iceberg while on its maiden voyage one cold night in April. The giant ship, 70,000 tons, 800 feet in length and with three thousand passengers aboard, was lost. Fourteen years later, the real *Titanic*, displacing 60,000 tons, 828 feet in length and with a passenger capacity of nearly three thousand, left England on its maiden voyage. On April 10th, it struck an iceberg and was lost. Both real and imaginary ships could make a speed of 24 to 25 knots, both had four funnels and three propellers, and both were short of lifeboats because they were considered to be unsinkable.

Herbert Greenhouse leaves it to the reader to judge whether Verne and Robertson were picking up psychic impressions of a future already determined, or if they were in some way impressing their fictional ideas on the future, moulding it so as to conform with their imagined scenarios – and before attempting to offer a conclusion here, I feel it helpful to examine further examples of such 'coincidences'. There is a particular event of this nature associated with the famous writer, Edgar Allen Poe, who in 1838 produced a novel called *The Narrative of Mr Pym*. In the story, Pym is involved in a shipwreck, being one of four survivors who manage to gain a lifeboat. Adrift for many days without food, they eventually decided to kill and eat one of their number, a cabin boy named Richard Parker. Arthur Koestler, the Hungarian-born novelist and writer of essays on parapsychology, reminds readers of this piece of fiction, adding an account related to him regarding an incident which took place in the summer of 1884. At that time, a relative of the person who told Koestler the story, was a cabin boy aboard a yawl named 'Mignonette' which foundered. There were four survivors who were adrift in an open boat for many days. In the end, desperate for food, they killed and ate the cabin boy – whose name was Richard Parker. Koestler terms this a 'pun of Destiny'.

Another example of the 'unknown' at work is the story of the Angels of Mons, a phenomenon which occurred in the autumn of 1914. The writer concerned in this instance was Arthur Machen, an unsuccessful novelist who had turned to acting as a second career. Soon after World War One had broken out, the *Evening News* approached Machen, commissioning him to write a short piece of 'heroic fiction', something to boost public morale and to offset the bad news from the battle front. He conceived a tale which he entitled *The Bowmen*, imagining an incident at Mons where St George of England, in shining armour at the head of his angels, who were in the guise of the old archers of the battle of Agincourt, came to the rescue of the beleagured British Army. It was published on the day after the retreat from Mons.

Unaccountably, the newspaper then received scores of letters from the battlefront, written by soldiers who swore on their honour that they had personally witnessed St George and his angels mingling in their ranks at the height of the engagement. Machen's story, they maintained, was not fiction, but truth. Many of the letters were published, exerting a profound influence on the readers of the *Evening News*. Dozens of times, Machen insisted that his story was pure invention, but no one believed him. With the advent of the Mons incident, he suddenly became a celebrity, and decided to return to writing as a full time occupation, hoping that the popularity which had previously eluded him would now materialise. But it was not to be, and he died in 1947 at the age of eighty four, with as little literary success as before. This is history as the general public knows it. There is, however, another aspect to the Machen saga, if the information supplied by Louis Pauwels and Jacques Bergier in *The Morning Of The Magicians* is to be relied upon. According to their research, Machen was a member of *The Golden Dawn*, a select group of occultists who met for the purposes of practising ceremonial magic and the acquisition of initiatory Hermetic knowledge. At the turn of the century it was rated as one of the most influential of Hermetic Orders. If Machen was indeed connected with this group, it would go a long way towards explaining the contents of a letter from Machen to the French writer, Paul-Jean Toulet, also quoted by Pauwels and Bergier. Referring to the fictional ideas in his own books, Machen wrote:

> When I was writing *The Great God Pan* and *The White Powder*, I did not believe that such strange things had ever happened in real life, or could ever have happened. Since then, and quite recently, I have had certain experiences in my own life which have entirely changed my point of view on these matters. . . . Henceforth I am quite convinced that nothing is impossible on this earth. . . .

Of some significance is the fact that this letter was penned in 1899, fifteen years before the advent of the Mons phenomenon.

Pauwels and Bergier also quote an instance where, after the death of the Austrian writer, Karl Hans Strobl, one of his close friends browsed through Strobl's library. In some of the writer's own works, the friend found a number of press cuttings secreted between the pages, and was startled to realise that they recorded events that Stobl had already described, long before they actually took place. It was natural for the friend to conclude that Strobl's writings contained an element of prophecy. But was it prophecy?

Three years before her death in 1924, the English novelist, Marie Corelli, wrote a book called *The Secret Power*, in which she described atomic energy and nuclear weapons with astounding accuracy. At the time, the theory of modern nuclear fission was in its infancy, as yet to be realised as an actuality. Natural radioactivity had been discovered in 1896, but it was not until 1939 that German researchers Hahn and

Strassmann found that uranium nuclei could be split, releasing huge amounts of energy in the heavy particles – the process we now know as 'fission'.

In Corelli's story, the character Gwent is made to dwell on the fact that the scientists of his world had made it possible for a single man to destroy a whole nation. He muses, recalling a passage that he had lately read in a book, concerning radioactivity:

> Radioactivity is an explosion of great violence; the energy exerted is millions of times more powerful than the highest explosive substance yet made in our laboratories; one bomb loaded with such energy would be equal to millions of bombs of the same size and energy as used in the trenches. One's mind stands aghast at the thought of what could be possible if such power were used for destructive purposes; a single aeroplane could carry sufficient to annihilate a whole army, or lay the biggest city in ruins with the death of all its inhabitants.

Gwent, who possesses the 'secret knowledge' of how this devastating power may be applied, intended to hand it over to one of the major world powers in exchange for the promise that it would be used to destroy any nation which attempted to go to war. As an Englishman, he wanted the information to be the property of his own country, but he had been snubbed by England's scientific fraternity, and therefore resolved to give it instead to America:

> Briefly – I offer the United States the power to end wars, and all thought or possibility of war.

As we are well aware, the gist of Marie Corelli's imaginative plot did materialise with uncanny accuracy.

In addition, the novel *Solution Unsatisfactory*, by the well known American science-fiction writer, Robert Heinlein, describes a Uranium 235 atom bomb, dropped by the United States on an enemy city in the closing stages of World War Two. Heinlein was subsequently investigated by F.B.I. agents, accused of 'disclosing top military secrets'. The charge was hastily dropped when it was shown that Heinlein's book was published in 1941, four years before the atomic raid on

Hiroshima. Far earlier, in 1927, the Russian novelist V. Nilolsky had written a story entitled *A Thousand Years Later*, in which he named 1945 as the year in which the first atomic explosion would take place.

In the 1880s, French novelist Albert Robida, gave his readers *War In The Twentieth Century*, telling of a war fought in 1945, with mines, submarines, torpedoes, smokescreens, aerial bombardment of cities and even with germ warfare.

The UFO phenomenon, at its peak during the '50s and '60s, nowadays commands appreciably less attention from the news media, although activity still takes place and is reported from time to time. I will not dwell on the reason why the phenomenon occurs, it having been comprehensively dealt with by Carl Jung. Of more interest and relevance here is the possible reason for its inception in the first place.

I refer to a resident of New England, USA, named William Denton. As early as 1866, Denton was proclaiming himself to be in telepathic contact with beings from another planet, eventually declaring that he and whole family had visited Mars and Venus. He wrote a series of privately published books on the subject, one of which was *The Soul Of Things*, wherein he described saucer-shaped space ships in great detail, saying that he thought they were constructed of aluminium. At that particular time, the concept of aluminium sheeting was a hopeful figment of the imagination, because although the metal had been isolated in 1827, a commercial process for the manufacture of aluminium was not invented until 1886.

As far as history records, Denton was the very first to project the image of a 'flying saucer', and from that point onwards, the whole spectrum of UFO phenomena began to build. At first, in the late 1890s, 'airships' were regularly reported to be seen in America, their occupants making brief if mysterious contact with humans. Later, came the emergence of the fully-fledged, saucer-shaped UFO, a subject which is familiar to all and requires no repetition here.

This apparent sequence of prophecy emanating from the works of certain writers has continued into the present day, one much publicised example being that of the novel, *Bloodsports*, by ex-jockey turned writer, Dick Francis. The theme of his plot depicted the kidnapping of a horse, a classic winner, for the purposes of ransom. In February 1983, a few years after the publication of Francis' book, the race horse Shergar was stolen from its stable in the Kildare countryside and was never recovered. Dick Francis believes it possible that his plot, as far-fatched as it is, gave the thieves the idea of holding a valuable horse to ransom.

Possibly. But let us apply the same deduction to the circumstances surrounding the death of Scots mountain climber turned novelist, Dougal Haston. In 1979 Haston wrote *Calculated Risk*, in which the central character, Jack McDonald, skis down a gully on the mountains above Leysin, a popular resort near Lausanne, and sets off an avalanche. In a hair-raising sequence, he skilfully skis out of its path to safety.

McDonald is portrayed as a veteran climber, the character bearing a strong resemblance to the author himself. Two months after completing the typescript, but before the book was actually published, Haston was skiing in the very same gully, in exactly the same conditions described in his book. There was an avalanche, but unlike his fictional counterpart, Haston was unable to outrun the falling snow and was engulfed.

The same uncanny element of foresight has been noticed in connection with the work of Manchester author, Richard Hugo, whose first book, *The Hitler Diaries*, was published in 1982, after four years of meticulous research. Less than a year after publication, the real life affair of the bogus Hitler Diaries uncannily mirrored the events depicted in Hugo's thriller. In 1983 he commenced work on another book, this time a disaster novel about a deadly radiation leak at a nuclear power plant in Russia. After three years of research, the novel was completed. It had only just been delivered to his London publisher when the Chernobyl disaster occurred.

Film scripts, too, are not exempt from such pre-vision. Subsequent to the making of Alfred Hitchcock's horror movie, *The Birds*, there were reports from several areas of unprecedented attacks on houses by flocks of birds – often crows, as in the picture. As an example, in June 1977, the owners of three hilltop bungalows in Fowlers Lane, Lightoaks village, Staffordshire, suffered daily bombardment against their windows by a large flock of angry crows, a series of attacks that lasted for more than a week, precipitating the unfortunate residents into a situation uncannily similar to that portrayed in the motion picture.

Of course, it is a well known fact that crows are territorial birds and if they catch sight of their reflection in a window they will invariably attempt to attack the image, but the scale and duration of the Lightoaks incident was much more than would normally be expected. So was it really a coincidence?

A more horrific event in its coincidental aspect was the fate of ten year old child acress, Judith Barsi, of Los Angeles, California. Pert, blonde and blue-eyed, Judith had appeared in such films as *Jaws IV, The Eye Of The Tiger*, and *Slam Dance*. She also had parts in the TV programmes *Cagney & Lacey, Growing Pains*, and *St Elsewhere*. Then she was cast in a highly rated TV film called *Fatal Vision*, the plot of which called for her to be murdered by her screen father. In the real life existence of the 1980s, Judith was one day murdered by her own father.

In November 1962 the motion picture, *The Manchurian Candidate*, opened in cinemas throughout the United States. The storyline tells of an American soldier in Korea, captured by the Communists and brainwashed. Then he is released and sent home to America to assassinate a Presidential candidate. In the film the assassin is played by English actor Laurence Harvey, the script calling for him to aim at his target through a window, high up in the convention hall. A year later, Lee Harvey Oswald, an ex-Marine who had once been in the hands of the Communists, shot President Kennedy to death in Dallas. Oswald fired at his target through a window, high up in a book depository.

Script writer George Axelrod remarked later that the coincidence of the name 'Harvey' was noticed almost immediately.

> 'I was in Paris,' he recalled, 'and within days there were pictures in the French press of Laurence Harvey together with Lee Harvey Oswald.'

But what of the coincidences that went unnoticed?

Frank Sinatra, who also acted in the film as a U.S. Army

officer, owned the copyright of the movie. So shocked was he at the uncannily prophetic way in which the filmed scenario had materialised in real life that he withdrew it and locked it away, releasing it only when the copyright expired in the Spring of 1988.

In response to a collection of incidents such as these – and I hasten to assure you that these are just a few of many more – the investigator can only ask himself the same question posed by Herbert Greenhouse. Are these cases of true prophecy – that is, correctly visualising events already established in future time and unchangeable, or is it evidence of the fact that the future can be created simply by the application of a vivid enough imagination powered by deep concentration?

In respect of the theory of prophecy, H.G. Wells was quick to admit that:

. . . the misses far outnumbered the hits. . . .

An honest answer; yet in *The World Set Free* (1914), Wells foresaw the energy crisis, atomic power, the advent of the kibbutz, and Pearl Harbour.

In the year nineteen eighty four, it was only to be expected that George Orwell's famous novel, *1984*, be reviewed to find out how much of his imagined future had come to pass since 1953, when he wrote it. Thankfully, not a great deal, although he had written of French measurement superceding the English. Decimal currency was envisioned, so was the widespread acceptance of films 'oozing with sex' – and his *Newspeak* and *double-think* have certainly materialised today in phrases like 'industrial action', which really means industrial inaction, or with 'army of liberation', more often than not proving to be an army of enslavement. These and other manifold examples are the language of the politician and union leader.

How is it, then, that only certain events can be 'foreseen' with accuracy?

I feel that the answer can be logically conceived if we begin by asking ourselves the following question: If future events are already patterned out for us as some think, and we have no alternative but to adhere to the pattern, what force is manufacturing the pattern and for what reason?

The fundamentalist will reply by quoting a personal philosophy which believes in an external, Supreme Being, a God who is 'guiding' the human race in its evolutionary journey towards the coming Golden Age. This view was widely held not so long ago, mainly by the uneducated, the superstitious, or by those too idle to attempt a discovery of the truth – a view which has been encouraged by the Church. The philosophy is flawed because it expects the supposedly 'divine' entity to think and react in a human manner – in a way that only results in the oft repeated questions; if the world is governed by an all-powerful, all-merciful God, as implied in the teachings of the Hebrew Prophets, why does he permit evil? Why in particular is it so often the case that the good suffer while the wicked prosper? Is it possible that belief in a Divine Providence which orders all things is a mockery and an illusion?

More rationally, the very fact that the act of positive thinking has been successfully practised by scores of people, as exemplified in the books of Al Koran, Normal Peale, Claude Bristol, Helen Rhodes-Wallace and others, indicates a different philosophy – that mankind can determine its own future merely by learning to understand and apply natural laws.

The mechanics of this act are not hard to understand, it simply requires an unprejudiced attitude of thought to begin with. To realise a desire in actuality – to make your wish come true – Peale gives the formula; prayerise; picturise; actualise.

> To assure something worthwhile happening, first pray about it. . . then print a picture of it in your mind as happening, holding the picture firmly in conscious-ness. . . .

Consider now what takes place in a writer's mind when he sits down to create a novel. He brings the characters to life in his imagination, 'seeing' their actions and circumstances over and over again, concentrating on the twists and turns of the plot over a period of time. The author's objective is to make his story as believable as possible to his readers – and here lies the crux of the mystery. The process of creating a fictional sequence and at the same time making it appear credible, demands of the writer a particular frame of mind. Firstly, however outlandish his scenario might be, it must be accepted in his mind as credible – that is, something that *could* happen in real life given the required circumstances. Secondly, having agreed with himself on its acceptability, the author must then think of it as having *already happened*, because only then can he go on to write of the consequences to his characters. If his visualisation and belief are strong enough, they emerge as positive thinking, the Hermetic practice, and therefore quite likely to impregnate the collective subconscious (the Matrix), in which case the imagined sequence is bound to manifest in reality. Perhaps we can all give thanks that the phenomenon only materialises on infrequent occasions.

Doubtless there is as great a reluctance to accept this concept as there is to believe that the stigmata of St Francis was a real event and not just some wild piece of fiction contrived by a religious fanatic. The alchemical writers of the past acknowledged the same *stumbling-block* – some in gentle terms, others more bluntly. Eliphas Levi, in *The Great Secret*, wrote

> This, then, at the outset, is a potent secret which is inaccessible to the majority of people – a secret which they will never guess and which it would be useless to tell them; the secret of their own stupidity.

If readers are prepared to accept that imaginative writers can, albeit unwittingly in most cases, exert such a powerful influence on segments of our collective future, then they may understand why the Hermetic process was called The Great Secret, and why the adepts were reluctant to openly discuss it. I have already had occasion to remark upon the unprecedented scope of allegorical literature, suggesting that it must inevitably have sprung from some profoundly important principle. I would assume that the manipulation of Destiny is reason enough.

It is also the reason why alchemists have stated categorically that it

> . . . has the power to pull down kings and princes. . . .

Khunrath in particular advised readers of his *Confession*:

> Therefore, fear God; what you seek is not little, but the greatest treasure of all. . . .

The great power of positive thinking is the reason why the events at Rennes le Chateau, as described in *The Holy Blood and the Holy Grail* emerged as they did to present all with an apparently unsolvable mystery. Within that saga, it was Louis Foquet who despatched an excitable letter to his brother Nicholas, then Superintendent of Finance at the court of Louis XIV, in which was penned this sentence:

> . . . nothing on earth could prove a better fortune, nor be its equal. . . .

There is an intriguing rider to this reference. Nicolas Foquet subsequently amassed a great deal of money under circumstances that were never made completely public. At the time, the official explanation rested with a charge of embezzlement, for which the King imprisoned Foquet. It was while serving his sentence that Foquet met the hooded prisoner around whom the 'man in the iron mask' legend grew. This mysterious prisoner, also incarcerated by order of the King, was allowed to communicate with no one – with the exception of Foquet. The import of this special exception from an ironclad rule, if viewed in light of the existence of Hermeticism, gives rise to the possibility of some fascinating speculation – but which we unfortunately cannot pursue here.

The influence which the minds of writers may have on the future of us all is mentioned at length here because the results can be readily compared with the original 'forecast', provided the literature in question has been preserved as evidence. But positive thinking, both on a large and small scale, does not rest solely in the hands of novelists. With the unwitting use of Doubt and Certainty, everyone holds the potential to exert a similar influence on the Matrix of life, the collective subconscious.

The human mind controls and directs the physical body's actions, making constant decisions regarding the pattern of everyday movement, whether to walk to the left or to the right, to do or not to do something, every decision being the result of either a long-planned intention, or a spur-of-the-moment impulse. Obviously, every action taken by a single individual is bound to affect others in some way or other, even though the effects are never fully appreciated. As a simple, local example, we may postulate a breakdown in transmission at a television station, causing certain programmes to be rescheduled to a later time in the evening. A teenage boy who wishes to see a particular programme stays up late to view it and consequently oversleeps the next morning, missing his paper round. A customer for the morning delivery fumes at the non-arrival of his paper, and on impulse, stops to buy one at another newsagent whilst driving to work. Having made his purchase, he then proceeds uneventfully to his destination. Had the breakdown at the television station not occurred, the boy would not have overslept, the man would have received his paper and thus lost no time on his way to work. He would have been driving past a particular point where, at that time, a child would have run into the road, chasing an errant ball. It is possible, therefore, to say that the breakdown at the television station saved the child's life, even though the two events were, to all intents and purposes, totally unrelated to one another. The fact is that all events are related to one another, and if a knowledgeable person can learn to influence this network of events, this skein of life, then it is apparent that the network can be influenced to the benefit of the influencer.

The concept of the eternal 'now', the Present Moment (the Matrix) is the hardest to grasp, especially for the newcomer to Gnostic philosophy, but it must be envisaged as a world-wide pattern of electrical impulses to which human minds constantly react, and which constantly reacts to human minds. This pattern of events is subject to alteration by fresh positive thoughts emitted from the minds of those who exercise the magic power of Certainty. All human thought is coloured by Certainty or Doubt, but such is our nature that with the constant application of the faculty called Reason, we tend to exercise Doubt far more than Certainty. It is a great relief, then, to know that a large percentage of human thought never impinges on the Matrix pattern. But when Certainty is successfully employed, the pattern is changed accordingly – and these changes, large or small, for the good or for the bad, are being wrought as every second of physical time ticks away. Thus, the Present Moment pattern is in a constant state of flux, with some portents for the future remaining stable while others change, either slightly or radically.

A correct grasp of this concept will bring enlightenment in regard to the mystery of so-called prophecy and prediction, for we tend to believe that the prophet can look ahead in time and actually 'see' an event scheduled to take place in the future – but this is not so. A prophet – a real psychic – is able to 'read' the state of the Present Moment pattern, the portents of which, *at the moment of prophecy*, indicate a certain sequence of events personal to the consulter of the prophet. Let us suppose that the prophet has 'seen' a future accident involving the consulter. The latter has two choices. He can either believe the prophet, or not. If he has been sufficiently impressed by the demeanour and mystique of the prophet and prophecy, it is possible that he will believe that the accident will indeed happen, and if he does, then he is thinking positively but to his own detriment, because there follows the possibility that his positive thought (Belief) will impregnate the Matrix, and the prophecy will certainly be fulfilled. But it is the consulter himself who has made sure that the prophecy is fulfilled, not Fate.

Alternatively, it may be perfectly true that the portents as read by the prophet do indicate an approaching accident, but the Matrix is subject to change, second by second, and it is quite possible that those influences which are leading to the accident will be changed before the event. If the consulter disbelieves the prophecy, he will be helping himself – especially if he *firmly believes* that the accident will not occur, for that belief is also positive and can have an effect on the Matrix. If you encounter a prophet, therefore, believe all the desirable things, but strongly disbelieve all the undesirables he may forecast. This view of the art of prophecy may explain why some predictions come true while others do not.

The most common of prophecies are those found in the newspapers and periodicals – the daily horoscopes, and I do not doubt that many have noticed that correct predictions rarely emanate from them, the reason being that it is simply not possible for the psychic to accurately 'see' events concerning a mass readership and then condense them into a few paragraphs of print. It will be argued that there are cases where horoscopes are fulfilled, and I concede that there are, at the same time reiterating that it is often the one receiving the prediction who makes it come true, or not, according to the *innermost belief* afforded it.

An extremely elementary method of foretelling the future is by use of a pendulum, consisting of a small object of your choice, like a ring or jewel, suspended on a length of thread. A cross is drawn on a piece of paper with the word 'YES' at the top of the vertical line, and 'NO' at one side of the horizontal. With the thread taken in between finger and thumb, the pendulum is suspended over the centre of the cross and a question asked of it. If the answer is in the affirmative, the pendulum will swing up and down the vertical line, seemingly not controlled by the one suspending it. If the answer is a negative, it will swing along the horizontal line, but if it is a 'don't know', the pendulum swings in a circle. Some practitioners of this form of divination will swear that, in many instances, the forecast they future accurately.

Agreed – but let the experimenter try this. Draw a cross with no 'yes' or 'no' and suspend the pendulum over it. Then visualise in your mind which way you would like the pendulum to swing. You will find that you will be able to direct which way it moves, vertically, horizontally, or in a circle, merely by exercising your imagination, and all without conscious volition. You will be especially successful if you *believe you can*. If, however, you hold unshakeable faith in the power of the pendulum to forecast future events, you will not be able to exercise control over the swing of it because that belief will affect the involuntary action of the muscles which give impetus to the direction of swing. As for accurately forecasting the future by this method, the same rules apply. The forecaster is 'reading' the Present Moment, and therefore the prediction will come true only if alternative influences injected into the pattern of the Matrix do not alter the portents.

Understandably, it places a great strain on credulity to ask acceptance of the fact that human thought alone, divorced from personal physical intervention, can dictate a future pattern of events – but if the pattern, the Matrix is conceived as I have described it, as a vast field of electrical impulses, then the illusion of material reality can be pushed aside, allowing the vision of a network of atoms. Can human thought influence and change atomic structure? Uri Geller does so every time he bends metal. I realise, however, that academics would prefer a more scholarly example and so I refer to a series of experiments which took place at Strasbourg University in the mid-sixties, under the direction of Professor Rémy Chauvin.

He used a Geiger counter to monitor radiation from an isotope of decaying uranium. Over a three minute period, the counter was stopped automatically at the end of every minute, while Chauvin's assistants were asked to focus mentally on the rate of isotopic decay, willing it to be accelerated during the first minute, and retarded during the second. Throughout the third minute, there was no mental will directed at the isotope. When the results were checked, it was discovered that the rate of disintegration had indeed been influenced by the mental commands. To check and double check, the experiments were repeated for two weeks, with different assistants, but still the results were positive.

Mankind in general will be reluctant to shoulder the whole responsibility for fashioning its own future, for it is one thing to accept that what you believe today will influence tomorrow, but quite another to find that what has happened today may have been the result of someone's imaginative thoughts of two, five, or ten years ago, and that what you think today will have an effect ten years hence.

Yet mankind's thoughts are his own remedy, if there is the urge to act collectively. Even the theosophical crusaders will agree with that. As Alice A. Bailey wrote, in *A Treatise On Cosmic Fire*:

> . . . a gigantic thought form hovers over the entire human family, built by men everywhere during the ages, energised by the insane desires and evil inclinations of all that is worst in men's nature and kept alive by the promptings of his lower desires. This thought form has to be broken up and dissipated by man himself. . . .

Chapter Seven

The Imagination is the second most powerful faculty of the human mind, for it pictures the ideas to which positive thinking will give ultimate reality. Yet the same power is often found to be leading the rational mind away from the truth rather than towards it, simply because imagination succumbs to personal desires and opinions, and nowhere is this better demonatrated than in the sphere of automatic writing, table rapping, or the Ouija board.

As long ago as 1917, Eleanor Sedgwick, at that time president of the Society for Psychical Research, attempted to warn against the trickery which a mind could play on itself. Although she believed in a survival after physical death, her comments in the Society's own Journal were hardly calculated to engender trust in the messages received through mediumistic 'communications'.

'Nobody,' she stated, 'should treat his own automatic writing, and still less communications through other mediums, whether private or professional, as oracle.'

Even if contact was made with a *communicator*, this could not guarantee a message coming through accurately.

'Our evidence, indeed, goes to show that it is often, if not always, adulterated by the automatist's own mind'.

In the seventy-odd intervening years between Eleanor Sedgwick's day and ours, experimental research has supported her misgivings, yet thousands still flock to witness theatre performances by present day mediums whose popularity is often comparable to that of a rock and roll idol. The reason why is not difficult to guess. It is because people are still searching for a sound philosophy, in desperate need to be assured that there is a continued life after death.

Modern research has uncovered the strange, dual nature of the brain, with the varied functions of the left and right hand lobes, showing that 'automatic' script (or the motivation of the Ouija board pointer) is ideo-motor activity emanating from what has been termed the 'alter-ego'. It is this mechanism which allows a free-running imagination to fabricate.

Almost everyone can receive 'spirit messages', providing they have the desire to do so, plus the patience to keep trying if at first attempt the phenomenon does not manifest. Most important of all requirements is the belief that contact can be made, and in the past, incentive to believe was provided by the thrilling prospect of communicating with the dead. One of the most radical instances of ideo-motor activity was that of an American dentist named John Newbrough. In 1882 he published a work entitled *Oahspe*, a volume produced by automatic typewriting. Its contents were remarkable. According to Newbrough's own account, he discovered quite early in life that he possessed a degree of clairvoyant ability. Often he found himself scribbling involuntary messages, either backwards or forwards, and could only regain control of his hands by forcing them away from the table. He also experienced visions and soon became deeply involved in an investigation of such phenomena, comparing notes with others subject to the same experiences. From them, he learned that his hands were being controlled by 'angels', and thus his conscious mind was further conditioned into an area of fantasy. After fifteen years of research, he concluded that he was failing to make full use of his marvellous powers and so embarked upon a rigid course of dietary discipline. He became a strict vegetarian, shunning all meat, fish, milk and butter, and taking to bathing twice a day as an exercise in purification. Each morning before dawn, he would rise and sit alone in a small room, meditating. Six years of adherence to this schedule reduced his weight from two hundred and fifty pounds to one hundred and eighty. He no longer suffered with rheumatic pain, or the headaches which had previously plagued him, and there was a marked enhancement of his paranormal ability in that he became clairaudient.

The time came when his voices instructed him to obtain a new invention of the period – a typewriter – and to learn how to use it, but after two years of practice, he achieved only moderate success. One morning, however, he awoke to find an inner impulse strongly urging him towards the machine, and once at the keyboard, his hands began to operate at great speed, entirely of their own volition. His voices directed him not to read what he had typed, but to repeat the process every morning thereafter. He obeyed, and at the end of fifty weeks' work, the typescript was declared complete. Still under the dictate of the invisible power, his hands drew a large number of illustrations which were to go with the book when it was submitted to a publisher. It emerged under the unlikely title of *Oahspe*, and without doubt – whatever you may think about Newbrough's story – is an enigma.

Its eight-hundred-odd pages are styled in a phraseology strongly reminiscent of the biblical texts, and are paragraphed in the same way. It is divided into Books, just as those of the Old and New Testament, but there the similarity ends.

The main portion of the text deals with the creation of Man, animals, plant life and the Heavens, a dissertation which occupies the first five hundred pages.

The most interesting section follows, the Book of Cosmogony and Prophecy, purporting to explain the true workings of the solar system and the entire Universe. I hardly need point out that its contents are at variance with the technical knowledge of today, to say nothing of philosophical thought.

A further section, the Book of Sephah, deals with the language of Pan; a vast continent which once occupied the area now covered by the Pacific Ocean. This language is a masterpiece of invention, its conception the province of a highly trained expert in languages, for it appears to be a combination of Hebrew, Greek, Latin, Chinese and Algonquin (a North American Indian dialect). It is claimed that John Newbrough, in his non-psychic mind, knew nothing of languages.

The Book of Cosmogony offers some unique ideas as alternatives to knowledge existing at the time. For example, it tells the reader that falling bodies do not plunge to the earth due to gravitational pull, but are pushed downwards by an outside force called Vortexya. Vortexya is an invisible force, very much the same as gravity, and which exists in everything. Each planet has its own Vortexya and it is the motion of such vortices, exerting a spiral force inwards towards a common centre which causes the formation of planetary bodies in the shape of a sphere. Earthly tides are caused by the fluctuating power of Earth's Vortexya and not by the gravitational pull of the Moon.

As the chapter unfolds, it turns further away from established knowledge, professing that the Sun does not reflect its light from the face of the Moon, but that the light of the Moon is actually a manifestation of the satellite's own Vortexya. Claiming that there is no such thing as light in the way that we conceive it, the book states that if Man were to view the Universe from a position outside the Earth's atmospheric lens, the Moon and the stars would not be visible, while the Sun would appear only as a pale red star. By virtue of the television pictures sent back from the surface of the Moon in 1969, even the lay person knows this to be false.

Sunspots, the book continues, are really dead planets which have lost their Vortexya and therefore cannot be seen by astronomers until they happen to drift between Earth and the Sun. Some of these planets, it is said, are barely a million miles out from Earth. Once again, we know this to be untrue.

The book is a treasure chest of other imaginative but entirely erroneous detail, so much so that the author's claim to have received it as an 'automatic' communication is wholly feasible.

In instances of ideo-motor 'communication' it has been noted that when the 'alter-ego' reaches the limits of the outer mind's actual knowledge of a subject, it will rarely be confined by those boundaries, but will almost certainly exceed them. What it doesn't know, it will invent, the object being in all cases to satisfy the wishes of the normal, waking mind. That is why, when the average adult sits down in front of an upturned wine-glass, or an Ouija board, he invariably receives messages from a deceased relative – say Auntie Mabel – who is now free from all her former suffering, happily residing in the Summerland with all her dear friends and favourite pets. Based on real entities in the subject's memory, they are nevertheless inventions of the 'alter-ego', brought into existence by the imagination so as to satisfy a need to know that there is a continued life after death, and that it will be comfortably familiar and pleasant. The more the subject *believes* the invention, the more detail will the imagination invent – and it is in this situation that the imagination is likely to overstep the mark. Discrepancies between actual fact and information offered as fact in the communications will be noticed, even by the most gullible. If, at that point, the subject can begin to question the discrepancies and actively *disbelieve* in the existence of a Summerland, or whatever form of 'heaven' is projected, then it will be found that the whole invention will disintegrate.

The mystifying contradictions which can arise from the workings of the 'alter-ego' are demonstrated in the life work of the American trance medium, Edgar Cayce, who on one hand consistently supplied correct diagnoses to sick patients, while on the other, offered them totally imaginative pictures of their past lives in Atlantis. Cayce was born in Kentucky in 1877, and as a seven-year-old, experienced paranormal visions of dead relatives. Later on, he attempted self-hypnosis in order to assimilate his more difficult lessons at school, but without much success. At the age of twenty one, he contracted advancing paralysis of the throat muscles, a malady which threatened the loss of his voice. When local doctors were unable to effect a cure, they resorted to hypnotism in the hope that it would succeed where conventional treatment had failed, but although the hypnotic suggestions seemed to disperse the condition, the symptoms recurred.

Intrigued by the experiment, Cayce asked a friend to hypnotise him and then suggest that he cure himself. Once in deep trance, Cayce's 'alter-ego' dictated a detailed medication and manipulative therapy that was to prove entirely successful.

A group of Kentucky physicians took advantage of this entranced diagnostic ability to cure the ills of other patients, soon discovering that Cayce, while hypnotised, need only be given the name and address of the patient, no matter where he, or she was, to be able to assume immediate mental contact and diagnose the true nature of the complaint. Cayce always maintained that his ability to perform this seemingly magical contact was through the medium of the Universal Mind (i.e. the Matrix).

The Sleeping Prophet, as he soon became known, began his

career of psychic diagnosis in 1910, and by the time he died in 1945, had amassed a collection of more than 14,000 stenographic records of his curative sessions. His successes were legion, his failures few – but the most controversial aspect of his 'readings' had nothing at all to do with medical treatment, for he would often digress unexpectedly into prophecy of important future events, or into a detailed description of a patient's past experience as a member of the race which populated the long lost continent of Atlantis. Thus there are today, on the files of the Association for Research and Enlightenment – an organisation founded to preserve and study the readings – many thousands of words relating to the history of Atlantis, its people and technology. The contents of those files show that, despite the undoubted accuracy of his diagnostic ability, Cayce, too, was subject to the whims of an unfettered imagination.

A substantial part of the readings have been collated in a volume entitled *Edgar Cayce on Atlantis* (1968), written by the medium's son, Edgar Evans Cayce. The early pages deal with the extremely distant past, at a time when Man was first projected on to Earth in his physical shape, a period which Cayce places at ten and a half million years B.C. As the chapters unfold, they portray the cultural rise of Atlantis, including three successive cataclysms which first broke the continent into several separate islands, and then finally submerged it beneath the waters of the Atlantic Ocean.

Naturally, such a sweeping and very much unsubstantiated concept has been the focus of considerable academic criticism, and it must be admitted that careful examination of certain readings will uncover some disturbing facts – disturbing, that is, for those who wish to believe in Cayce's picture of the past. For example, in July 1925, reading number 2665–2 informed one patient that he had experienced a previous life some ten million years ago, when he lived in an area now known as New Mexico. Even today, it was said, there may still be seen in the ruins and caves of the north western part of this area, some rock drawings made by the entity in that remote time. We must now compare this proposition with the information that the Doheny Archaeological Expedition, while searching the Hava Supai Canyon in northern Arizona, discovered a rock painting dating from extremely remote times. While unusual in itself, the most intriguing aspect of the discovery was that the painting depicted a standing Tyrannosaurus, an animal that had previously been presumed extinct long before the appearance of Man. The find suggested that this variance required either the extinction date of the animal to be advanced, or the date of Man's advent to be put back. As would be expected, such a thought-provoking discovery soon became the subject of national publicity. It may be recalled by some that the Doheny Expedition took place in 1924, and thus the painting was found almost a year before Cayce described an amazingly similar situation in his reading. Even the area is compatible, for the Hava Supai Canyon is not too far removed from north western New Mexico.

Setting aside any thoughts of deliberate deception – I do not suggest that for one moment – it leaves the feeling that Cayce's imagination, free and unfettered while in trance, made opportune use of an existing fact to concoct a fantasy.

A review of Cayce's information about the great culture of Atlantis will reveal that its people had invented ships, cars, submarines and aeroplanes. More especially it had the technological advantages of radio and television transmissions, and of powered vehicles which were motivated by 'beamed' inductive energy – the latter idea being the most interesting of all and being dealt with at some length. Collection and distribution of this 'beamed' power was achieved by means of a giant, man-made crystal, cut with angled facets in such a way that the rays of the sun were focussed into high concentration. The resulting energy was then broadcast, in the same way that a present day TV signal is transmitted, to be picked up by the machines which utilised it.

Modern science, with the sources of energy an important priority, has given consideration to the idea of inductive power, but as yet with only moderate and profitless success. It is readily appreciated that the general concept, as described by Cayce, is identical to the technology of the laser and maser, the amplification of light and microwaves by beaming them through a ruby. Those who believe unreservedly in Cayce's Atlantean lore are quick to point out that the earliest reading which mentioned the crystal was given in 1933, long before the appearance of the first workable laser. Quite so, but evaluation of information received through an entranced subject is not quite so simple as that. The same temporal factors that were brought to your attention in the previous chapter must apply here. In this case, the date to be most strongly considered is that at which the idea was *first conceived* in the minds of men, not that at which the end product materialised in reality.

In addition, it is imperative to consider the period in which Cayce had spent his life, thus far, and the influences to which he might have been subjected. He would have been eleven years old at the time Ignatius Donnelly published his extremely popular and thought-provoking book, *Atlantis*, a work which excited the imagination of readers everywhere. In the wake of such a popular publication, it was inevitable that others would follow, to enlarge on the idea, or to present alternative views. One such volume was the 1899 publication of *A Dweller On Two Planets*, by Frederick S. Oliver. In something of the style of John Newbrough, Oliver claimed his work to have been the result of mental conversations with an entity called Phylos, who manifested as a clairvoyant voice, and who dictated the text of the book.

The opening segment was set in an Atlantis of 12,000 B.C. and it is significant to note that certain ideas expressed therein are forerunners of those later presented by Cayce. As an example, it is reported that the capital city of Atlantis is Caiphul:

> . . . wherein tubes of crystal, absolutely exhausted of air, gave continuous light derived from the 'Night-Side' forces. . . .

To the believing mind, this may present a picture of some great crystal emitting light as a result of some force unknown to modern science – although if one cares to consider ordinary electricity as a force drawn from the 'Night-Side' of nature (a term also used by Cayce), the 'crystal tubes' can be more reasonably viewed as common electric light bulbs.

A better example may be found in the description by Phylos of the mysterious Maxin Stone, a phenomenon which resided in an especially sacred part of an Atlantean temple. There, in the centre of the floor, stood a large block of crystal, a perfect cube in shape and on top of which rested the Maxin.

> This seemed aflame, in shape like a giant spearhead, and it cast a light of intense power over all things around, yet no one could look at its steady, unwavering white glow without desiring shade for the eyes. . . . Over three times the height of a tall man it stood, a mysterious manifestation of Incal (God), as all spectators believed. In reality, it was an occult, odic light, and had stood in that one spot for centuries.. . . . It made no heat, did not even warm the quartz pedestal; yet for any living being to touch it was fatal in the instant of the rash act. No oil, no fuel, no electric currents fed it; no man touched it.

This compares admirably with Cayce's description of his own giant crystal – the firestone – housed within a domed powerhouse, but the latter part of the same reading offers a far more interesting comparison. Asked a specific question about Atlantis, Cayce spoke in particular of a special stone, the forerunner of the specially cut ruby crystal, known to early Atlanteans as the 'Tuaoi Stone'. When asked to state its use, the seer replied that it was a 'white stone by means of which the Atlanteans communicated with the Universal Consciousness' (again the Matrix). He further described it as a six-sided figure in which the light appears as a means of communication. In an effort to determine exactly what this strange piece of stone might be, many have sought to rationalise it as some sort of special crystal akin to those which seers are popularly supposed to look into. Yet the expositions given in the two previous volumes have shown that the 'white stone' mentioned in Revelation 2, 17, is fundamentally the same as the Philosophers' Stone of the alchemists, the Hermetically enhanced understanding – which can indeed communicate with the Universal Consciousness. Could Cayce be speaking of this instead of a mere crystal ball?

From the description of the Tuaoi Stone's shape, there can be two possible interpretations in an allegorical light. The most famous of signs connected with the Hermetic scheme, the six-pointed Star of David, has all the necessary qualifications. So, too, has the cube, a six-sided figure – and as

Cayce was discussing a white stone, we could conclude that he was referring to the figurative 'cube' of the Temple of Solomon. This also, is symbolic of the Hermetic understanding as the 'finished stone'.

The relationship may seem tenuous, but Cayce gave an even broader hint when he was asked if it were possible for Man to know again the secret of the Tuaoi Stone. This information, the entranced seer replied, may not wholly be given through any channel until the individual had *purified his purposes and desires*. The questioner, unable to make any sense of this, wanted to know the nature of the purification, to which Cayce answered that the inner self must be purified in the same way as the soul is purified in between appearances on Earth. In other words, the inner consciousness must attain the same state as that of the Universal Mind – shorn of all false human beliefs and with an enhanced understanding.

It is not hard to agree that the Maxin Stone and the Tuaoi Stone are imaginative representatives of the same principle.

Another intriguing discovery is that an anagrammatical form of the name 'Tuaoi' appears in *The Secret Doctrine*, the work written by Madame Blavatsky in 1888. Discussing an item from the *Egyptian Book of the Dead*, she writes:

> For what is *Tiaou*? The frequent allusion to it in the 'Book Of The Dead' contains a mystery. *Tiaou* is the path of the Night Sun, the inferior hemisphere, or the infernal region of the Egyptians, placed by them on the *concealed side of the moon*. The human being, in their esotericism, came out from the moon (a triple mystery – astronomical, physiological, and physical at once); he crossed the whole cycle of existence and then returned to his birthplace before issuing from it again. Thus the defunct is shown arriving in the West, receiving his judgement before Osiris, resurrecting as the god Horus, and circling round the sidereal heavens, which is allegorical assimilation to Ra, the Sun; then having crossed the *Noot* (the celestial abyss), returning once more to Tiaou. . . .

In this wholly allegorical representation, it is apparent that *Tiaou* is merely an alternative name for the more often applied

Tuat – the abode of the dead, i.e. the Universal Consciousness, or whatever else you may find it called.

Having discovered this underlying connection, we may further investigate Cayce's data on Atlantis, coming to the point where, in 1968, the story took a dramatic turn. Pilots of light aircraft in the area of the Bimini Islands and the Island of Andross, parts of the Bahamas Group, began to report sightings of strange underwater constructions. Subsequent investigation, both by air and under water, has revealed nearly forty square miles of sunken ruins which, some generously estimate, date from the end of the last Ice Age, about 10,000 B.C. A number of writers immediately pointed out that as early as 1933, Edgar Cayce had forecast that Atlantis would 'rise again', to be discovered in this very same area. In 1940, he named the precise year in which the discovery would be made: 'Expect it in '68 and '69.' Thus the appearance of the ruins seemed indisputably to qualify Cayce's talent as a seer. But let us carefully consider certain facts. As with practitioners of the Ouija board, or the up-turned wine glass, the imaginative fantasies woven by the mind while in a trance such as that into which Cayce regularly descended, are reflections of the interests, knowledge – and more importantly – speculative beliefs held by the waking mind. The more intense the interest in any specific subject, the more creative the fantasy during the time the imagination is uncoupled from the restraint of reason (and Doubt).

Cayce had a special interest in the Bimini area which began as early as 1926, when he was approached by a man who asked him to use his psychic powers to locate oil in Florida. Cayce obliged, and during the course of many such readings, there emerged information relating to a buried treasure. What took place then, only the Cayce records can divulge, but it is known that the oil man disappeared, never to be heard from again. In 1927, Cayce himself visited Bimini. While there, he doubtless absorbed local tradition concerning the Islands' past, and although what he learned is not recorded, it is safe to say that it set the scene for the 1933 prediction that the remains of Atlantis would be discovered there. The forecast was strengthened in 1935, when Cayce discussed Bimini with a young aviatrix who came to him for a reading, and who at his suggestion, flew there in order to search for an ancient freshwater well now covered by the sea, but supposed to be visible at certain low tides. It is reported in the A.R.E. records that the woman ultimately located the well beneath the waterline of the south-east shore of North Bimini. She indicated that it was of extremely ancient date and that it was walled round with a peculiar type of stone on which were carved strange symbols. This apparent verification of fisherfolk lore served to fuel Cayce's waking interest in the subject of Atlantis, which in turn added impetus to the creativity of his imagination when entranced.

Certainly the discovery date of the underwater ruins coincided with that given by Cayce in 1940 for the rising of Atlantis, and we might interpret this as true predictive power. But what actually has been discovered?

As I have already sought to make clear in *Hermes Unveiled*, Plato's description of Atlantis, an account upon which all subsequent books on the subject are based, is a fable especially contrived in order to covertly present the Hermetic knowledge, the old secret of positive thinking. What has been discovered in the Bahamas, therefore, cannot be Atlantis, but is no more than some old ruins that were once above the water line in a relatively recent era of the past, and certainly not as far back as 10,000 B.C. The 'mysterious' symbols carved into the wall of the freshwater well have their counterpart not far away in the jungles of Yucatan, where many examples of Mayan sculpture are to be seen. There is even doubt in the minds of some scholars about certain of the 'ruins', for one opinion is that they are freak formations, naturally eroded into shapes that cause them to appear as blocked out by human hands.

It is conceded that many will argue this point, and not a few who will disagree with this evaluation of the Cayce phenomenon. The same sharp difference of opinion exists in regard to the phenomenon of hypnotic regression, an alternative but nevertheless near-identical manifestation of the imaginative powers. They are inventions, notwithstanding the appearance of uncanny accuracy in certain cases.

The question arises; why is it that the mind will go to such lengths to deceive? If Cayce could diagnose ills and recommend cures with such startling accuracy – and there is no doubt about that – why was the same reliability absent from his pictures of the past? Why resort to invention, no matter how wonderfully creative it was?

Part of the answer lies in an understanding of basic human desires and beliefs, applicable in both aspects of the seer's work. When a patient came to Cayce to be healed, it was generally because orthodox medicine had failed to bring about a cure, and the Sleeping Prophet was the last resort. Therefore, a strong desire to be cured, coupled with a belief in the healer's reputation already existed in the patient's mind. Add to that Cayce's own strong belief in his curative ability, a belief which had been awakened early in life and had grown into a manifestation of power akin to that of John Keely but of an alternative nature, and which had continued to strengthen with each successful diagnosis. Cayce *knew* he could heal and knew the patient wanted to be healed. As for the subject of reincarnation and of long lost Atlantis, there is no doubt at all that it was of consuming interest to the waking mind of Cayce, and as such would be bound to emerge in any situation where the imagination would find itself free of reason and doubt, i.e. in trance. The subject of Atlantis, like that of Jesus, is strangely emotive to many people. They *want* to believe in it. When a patient with a similar interest in the lost continent questioned Cayce about it, that person's basic desire was not necessarily to be told the truth, for the truth is often unpalatable. Rather the inner desire was to be assured that the great Atlantean culture did once exist, and that there was personal association with it – and so Cayce's 'alter-ego' obligingly told them what they most wanted to hear. It was what Cayce wanted to hear, too, when he came out of the trance. This is only basic human nature – it loves a mystery and would rather associate with a mystery that appears unsolvable, for once the answer is found, it is robbed of the feeling of mystique. People are content to believe in Atlantis, just as others are willing to believe in the second coming of Christ, or of the existence of a highly advanced technological culture watching over us by means of their UFOs. The same mechanism pictures Aunt Mabel in idyllic Summerland, a form of mental balm that does no real damage unless it becomes obsessive. That it is fallible is demonstrated only too clearly in those instances where advice received from entranced sources can be checked at the time – as in the readings where Cayce gave locations of buried treasure, or of a vein of gold ore. Despite meticulous and repeated directions given in relation to several different hidden hoards, none was ever found. Why does the imagination behave in this way? Frankly, because its principle function is to create the future, not read the past, or the present. When it is not motivated by reason, or by positive thinking in the act of impregnating the Matrix, it becomes like a ship at sea with no engine to drive it. It will drift superbly, but aimlessly. Try to imagine the past outside your scope of knowledge, or an alternative *now*, and you will imagine fiction.

Outside the Hermetic framework, clearly the most impressive use of the imagination was by the Austro-Hungarian engineer, Nikola Tesla. An electrical genius, he was responsible for many inventions, including the polyphase alternating current system of power supply in use today. He formulated the theory of how to transmit power without the use of cables, thus almost bringing Cayce's vision of inductive energy to reality, and demonstrated that power could be drawn from the earth anywhere merely by making a connection to the ground.

His mental gifts included the ability to imagine an object with such clarity that, to him, it appeared as almost a reality. This allowed him to construct the prototype of the first alternating current motor without resorting to the drawing board, for he 'saw' each part more vividly than it would have been on a blueprint, and calculated each dimension so exactly that there was no need to test them by partial assembly. There was no question of them being imperfect in fitting. And the finished article, Tesla noted, was *exactly as he had visualised it one year previously*.

In regard to his ability to visualise, Tesla revealed that, in his boyhood he had not understood it, looking upon it as an affliction rather than an attribute. He recalled that:

> When a word was spoken, the image of the object designated would present itself so vividly to my vision that I could not tell whether it was real or not. . . . Even

though I reached out and passed my hand through it, the image would remain fixed in space.

Encouraged by his mother, Tesla attempted to banish the images, using the faculty against itself by imagining that they weren't there. The visions always returned, however, and in the end he made use of them for his own pleasure, embarking upon countless journeys to new places, cities and countries, even making imaginary friends to whom he became strongly attached. At the age of seventeen, however, he decided to apply his power to the sphere of serious invention. As early as 1890, he had created a 'magic light' – vacuum tubes that were lit by a high frequency oscillator and entirely unconnected to the power source by wires. Could this have been the reality which inspired Frederick Oliver and Edgar Cayce in their imaginative scenarios?

Tesla had no religious beliefs – not in the sense projected by the Church – but his philosophy of later years has a familiar ring. He acknowledged the existence of a primary substance which is acted upon by a creative force, thus calling into existence all material things, pondering the evolution of Man's mind, whether he could learn to control this awe inspiring creative process of Nature:

> To create and annihilate material substance, cause it to aggregate in forms according to his desire, would be the supreme manifestation of power in Man's mind, his most complete triumph over the physical world, his crowning achievement which would place him beside his creator, make him fulfill his ultimate destiny.

The comparison between Tesla and others who have experienced manifestations of the subconscious power – uselessly in the cases of Keely and Geller, beneficially in those of Rudder and Traynor – is of great interest. Biographical information concerning Tesla does not indicate an association with any Hermetic fraternity. It seems that, from early childhood, he had achieved much of what the true Hermeticist seeks to develop, and it is without question that he was born with the transmission of consciousness already accomplished.

Chapter Eight

In *The Holy Blood and the Holy Grail* (1982), Henry Lincoln and his co-authors reminded readers of the growing dissention within the Roman Catholic Church, quoting in particular the outspoken comments by Archbishop Marcel Lefebvre against Pope Paul VI. In 1976 and 1977 Lefebvre was threatened with excommunication, but at the last moment the Pope relented, in the belief that Lefebvre was being 'manipulated' by some faction intent on creating argument within the Church. Lincoln quotes an excerpt from *The Guardian*, dated August 30th 1976, at the height of the argument:

> The Archbishop's team of priests in England . . . believe that their leader still has a powerful weapon to use in his dispute with the Vatican. No one will give any hint of its nature, but Father Peter Morgan, the group's leader . . . describes it as being 'earth-shaking'. . . .

Lincoln, naturally intrigued by this implication, wrote directly to Father Morgan, but received no reply. Thus, for Lincoln, the mystery remained. However, let us couple this item with a small quotation made by Eliphas Levi, in *The Great Secret*:

> The Catholic religion keeps its hold on the masses by a secret unknown to the Pope himself. . . .

Both statements are provocative, being the cause of much wonder and speculation as to what this 'earth-shaking' secret might be. Yet the answer can only be Gnosticism (Gnosis), that old arch-enemy of Vatican philosophy and champion of the creative ability of Self. Throughout this whole work, I have endeavoured to emphasise the fact that Belief is a potent force, and to draw attention to this eternally active power which governs and dictates all our attitudes in material life. Belief is virtually the Life Force.

Every waking moment, the minds of men and women are

continually open to the power of suggestion, as any hypnotist will confirm, and so our opinions, prejudices, likes, dislikes, customs and habits are formed more on the basis of what others around us believe, rather than as a result of individual reasoning. In many instances we copy the beliefs of others without question, simply because we cannot bring ourselves to believe in an alternative. Therefore, in a peculiar way, belief is like a contagious virus – and never more so than in relation to religion. Whereas it is easy to agree that the custom of using a knife and fork at the table has some merit, although it is only essential as long as we believe so, it is less easy to agree upon answers to such questions as: is there a God? why are we here? what is the purpose of life? is mankind free to shape each his own destiny, or is all that exists governed by random chance?

Self-analysis and the development of the understanding, being the key to obtaining the answers, demand considerable time and strength of purpose – far more, in fact, than most are prepared to give.

Nevertheless, a few here and there in every generation manage to achieve a deeper appreciation of the way in which Nature operates, and having done so, are eager to pass on this understanding to others – but it is at this point that the classic *stumbling-block* is encountered. How does one convey knowledge from a developed understanding to one that has not been developed? The blunt answer is that it is not possible, unless the underdeveloped are prepared to accept the teaching. In the case of those who have already reached maturity, it may be asking too much, for by then, their minds may be already preconditioned to whatever philosophy they have been exposed to. To discard all this for the principles outlined here would require on their part, a radical change of belief.

In the past, those who attained Gnosis (Wisdom) wrote down, or preached their knowledge in a form that would be most attractive to non-initiates – that is, by means of parable, allegory, nursery tales and fairy stories, in the hope that some would read or listen with more than just a superficial interest. The move was successful in that individual texts attracted particular devotees, small groups, the members of which were themselves on the threshold of enlightenment and were determined to discover the core of the teaching hidden behind the literal word. In time, these groups grew larger, enjoined with followers who were less enlightened and who argued against the idea of a secret teaching, preferring instead to place emphasis on the literal word of each text. Thus were 'religions' born, developing in all nations, either in accordance with belief in the literal, or with belief in the secret teaching. Thus, two basic religions have grown up side by side. One is a philosophy based on the belief that 'God' is in the individual's own mind and that if he or she learns how, control of one's destiny can be achieved by means of the Hermetic process. The followers of this scheme are known as Gnostics, Hermeticists, Alchemists, Rosicrucians, and in these modern times, as Positive Thinkers.

The other philosophy places belief in the literal meaning of the religious and alchemical texts, maintaining that God is external to Man. These are the Fundamentalist Christians, Catholics, Protestants and all the other denominations.

The followers of the latter group have been taught, in the form of a belief handed down to them over the centuries, that in order for them to converse with God, or to receive any beneficial influence therefrom, it is essential to place one's faith in the Church and its clergy as an intermediatory between man and spirit. Many Catholics, for example, consider the Pope to be only one step removed from the Divine Himself.

The Gnostic, on the other hand, knows that no man is any more divine than another, and that each and every human has a personal inlet to 'God', the subconscious miracle power, by merely adopting the correct frame of mind.

I would sincerely hope that this distinction, with all its ramifications, will prove enlightening in relation to the 'earth-shaking' secret of Levi and Lefebvre. The term 'earth-shaking' is itself a blatant use of an allegorical code word, meant to indicate a *radical change of belief*.

Since its inception, the Roman Catholic Church has always held that Gnosticism is heresy, and indeed, accounts of persecution inflicted by the Church upon Gnostics are graphic and numerous. Yet the supreme irony lies in the fact that the Old and New Testament documents upon which the

Christian religion is founded, were written by Gnostics. St Paul, too, was a Gnostic, as is clearly indicated in his 'letters', provided one can recognise the statements intended to convey such information.

The Gnostic (from the Greek *Gnostikos* – significantly *knowing*) does not dedicate his life to the acquisition of intellectual knowledge (knowledge held in the memory) but to intuitive understanding, rightly maintaining that Gnosis that can be taught is not true Gnosis. Carl Jung, the noted psychologist, became a Gnostic. With regard to Church doctrine, he wrote:

> Only fools attach to dogma, but what is necessary now is that we understand it in a new way, namely not as a hundred percent truth, but as a symbol.

In an interview filmed towards the end of his life, Jung created a sensation with his answers to a particular line of questioning concerning his religion:

> Interviewer: Did you believe in God?
> Jung: Oh, yes.
> Interviewer: Do you *now* believe in God?
> Jung: Now? . . . (long pause) . . . Difficult to answer . . . I know . . . I don't need to believe . . . I know.

Afterwards, Jung was inundated with letters from people asking what it was he knew. The answer is that he never doubted that there was something which, for the want of a better term, people call God. One aspect of Gnosticism is the unchallenged equality of women, for women have the same inlet to the subconscious as men if they choose to use it, but mediaeval Catholicism saw this as heresy, the factor being one of the main reasons why the Cathars, a sect sprung out of Gnostic teaching, were persecuted and eventually subjected to the Inquisition of the 13th century.

Today, the same issue is the cause of a major disagreement in the Church of England, latterly of such magnitude that it threatens to cause an irrevocable division. Although the subject of the ordination of women has been one of contention for some time, the matter was precipitated early in 1984, in New York, when Edwina Sandys, one of Sir Winston

Churchill's grand-daughters, revealed to the Very Reverend James Park Morton, Dean of the Episcopalian cathedral of St John the Divine, that she owned a bronze statue depicting Christ as a woman. After some discussion, Bishop Morton agreed to display the figure in his cathedral during Holy Week. The four foot high bronze shows a female figure in Christ's crucified position, but without the Cross. The reception afforded the display was mixed, some traditional worshippers claiming that they had experienced Holy Week in a new way, due to the presence of the statue. Others, however, were scandalized, including Morton's superior, Bishop Walter Dennis, Episcopal Suffragan Bishop of New York, who declared himself shocked, condemning the figure as 'theologically and historically indefensible'.

What started as a vociferous disagreement became no less than an international furore in 1986, the focus this time being the tiny parish church of St Michael's in Tulsa, Oklahoma.

St Michael's, a suburban Episcopalian church with a congregation of no more than a hundred, became the scene of a protracted dispute between its rector, Father John Pasco, and the Bishop of Oklahoma – a simmering argument which culminated in Father Pasco being unfrocked. Publicly, the Bishop maintained that the dispute concerned no more than church property and discipline, but Father Pasco let it be known that the roots of the matter lay in his own strong traditionalist beliefs, including opposition to women priests. What began as a purely local argument developed into an international furore when Father Pasco contacted Doctor Graham Leonard, Bishop of London and third in the Church of England hierarchy, requesting that the Tulsa church be in communion with him.

Although no English bishop had involved himself in American church affairs since the War of Independence, Dr Leonard, a strong opponent of the ordination of women, agreed. Ignoring a request from no less a person than the Archbishop of Canterbury, Dr Robert Runcie, Dr Leonard made arrangements to fly to Tulsa and hold a confirmation service at St Michael's.

By February 26th 1987, the day on which the General Synod cast their votes for or against the introduction of women priests, the affair had reached a stage where it seemed that the entire Church of England would be divided on the issue, so much so, some felt, that two separate Churches might emerge.

Dr Leonard's point of view is that of the simple Fundamentalist. He believes implicitly in the historicity of Jesus, averring that events recorded in the Gospels are literal fact. He is quoted as saying that:

> The church exists as an unalterable truth, which it is itself now proposing to alter. That truth took place in the first century in Palestine when God chose to take on human flesh as a *man*. . . . The way he chose to do this as a man and not as a woman should be reflected in the ministry of the church.
>
> (Daily Mail, Feb 19th 1987)

The alternative view is stated by the Right Reverend David Jenkins, Bishop of Durham. Writing in his diocesan news letter, he suggests that it is 'increasingly unsatisfactory' to refer to God constantly as 'He'.

> Clearly, God is not exclusively male. He (she) must reflect all that is female. . . .

In light of Gnostic knowledge, the gross incongruity of this furore, where both sides are arguing out of sheer ignorance, is astounding and is beyond further comment here.

A similar point of dispute, although much less heated, was raised at the General Synod in York during July 1987, following a report submitted by a seven-member team investigating Freemasonry. After a year of study, the team – which included two Masons – attacked the Craft's rituals, claiming them to have 'psychic effects' upon some Christians. Certain sections of the ritual were described as 'blasphemous' and 'positively evil'. The report stated that

> Some Christians, themselves once Freemasons, have left the Craft precisely because they perceive their membership of it as being in conflict with their Christian witness and belief.

Not unexpectedly, the United Grand Lodge deplored the

condemnation of part of the Masonic ritual as blasphemous, maintaining that it would have been unthinkable for early Freemasons to have designed or taken part in a system which was in any way blasphemous or heretical. There is a certain amount of incongruity here too, for, as I have taken pains to demonstrate in *Hermes Unveiled*, traditional Masonic ritual is founded on Hermetic symbolism. To put it more bluntly, it too was designed by Gnostics to promote the Great Secret of positive thinking, just as the Gospels were.

Dissention on this particular subject has been long running, even within the Masonic structure itself. Madame Blavatsky, in *Isis Unveiled*, reported a typical exchange of views, first from the Supreme Councils of the Ancient and Accepted Rite at Lausanne, in the late 1800s, which announced:

> Freemasonry proclaims, as it has proclaimed from its origin, the existence of a creative principle, under the name of the Great Architect of the Universe.

Christian traditionalists, however, countered this by replying that:

> . . . belief in a creative principle is not the belief in God, which Freemasonry requires of every candidate. . . .

From the Gnostic point of view, there is little to choose between the Church or Freemasonry. The Church attracts its membership by promotion of the belief that the Crucifixion and the Resurrection were real events, and by preaching that as God manifested in the flesh then, so He may do so again, and it is wise to be spiritually prepared. Thus, the Church acts as a world wide counselling service to which the intuitionally unaware can attach themselves and draw reassurance about the hereafter. An elaborate system of ritual, plus the adoption by the clergy of grandiose titles helps to sustain the belief of 'the faithful'.

Slightly more in line with reality, Freemasonry is a world wide social club which, like the Church, is well known for its charitable acts. It attracts membership on two counts, firstly because of the mystique of its supposedly secret initiation ritual and recognition signals, but mainly because of the undoubted benefits afforded to brother from brother, to the exclusion of outsiders. Thus, it capitalises on a basic human trait – partisanship, or 'protectionism' as it is lately called.

Much of the membership of both factions seem unaware that their 'clubs' are founded on the Gnostic (Hermetic) principle, the original intention being the transmission of the knowledge of positive thinking. As for the true Gnostic, if the Hermetic process is undertaken and achieved, he has no need of any 'club' at all, although it must be said that some do exist in a covert manner.

In the early '60s, writer Arkon Daraul devoted a segment of his book, *Secret Societies*, to a description of the Cult of the Peacock Angel, whose members, he reports, met once a fortnight in an underground temple in Putney, south London.

They paid homage to an eight-feet tall, glossy black statue of a peacock, the feet of which rested in a pool of *water*, and before which the cult members danced, each one robed in a flowing *white* smock that entirely covered their ordinary clothes. On the breast of each robe was embroidered the figure of a peacock, some coloured *red, black*, or *green*. Another emblem used by them was the *snake*, but there was nothing evil or sinister in their lodge rites. The membership were trained to believe that there were two powers which can help them in everyday life, the power of increase and the power of construction, both of which were referred to by secret names which themselves represented the *peacock* and the *snake*.

The main object of the lodge was to induce an ecstatic experience that would 'disassociate the mind from the body', so that at a certain point in development, the worshipper became 'enlightened'. The rites were also designed to aid members in a material sense, by the *instilling of confidence* in a specific objective. A mind training programme was designed to lead the candidate towards a 'mystical' experience, partly induced by the conscious exercise of the emotions at will. Required of every candidate was implicit belief in the existence of peacock power.

It required little deductive effort to categorise this as a Gnostic cult, for Hermetic symbolism is present here, denoted by the emphasised words. The Peacock is an age old Hermetic symbol, employed because of the distinctive markings on its fanned tail. In mythology, Argus was a character who had eyes all over his body and was known as the god of magic. When Hermes slew him, Hera placed all his eyes in the peacock's tail. Thus, as Argus represented the all-seeing (i.e. all-*knowing*) wise man, so does the peacock symbol.

The Peacock cult, it is said, was brought to London in 1913, by a Syrian, who established the initial lodge. It prospered and the cult spread until sixteen lodges existed. From the above description it can be plainly seen that the principle of positive thinking was its foundation stone, whilst the elaborate ritual was, as ever, designed to focus the candidate's belief.

Apparent, too, is the likelihood that the Syrian who introduced the cult to England was a Sufi, the Persian counterpart of the Gnostic, and identical in philosophy. This sect does not ordinarily seek converts, for in the countries where Sufism is deeply rooted, there is no lack of applicants.

Orthodox Western religions will not endorse Sufi teachings because they are designed to set the neophyte free from the restrictive psychology of established religious beliefs. As one very minor example, the Sufis do not preach celibacy as a requisite to reach God. The Sufi masters assume that a certain nobility of mind and purpose resides within every human being and it is their task to discover and develop it. Theirs is a philosophy of great positiveness and there exists a belief that the higher echelons of the Sufis, the real adepts, can influence the minds of men and manipulate events in a totally inexplicable manner. But I trust that, by now, the reader will no longer find the idea quite so inexplicable.

One incredible facet of Sufi lore, which I take the opportunity to explain at this point, is that which declares the need to change the past before the future can be altered.

At first appraisal, this proposition would appear to be an impossible paradox, an absurd and mystical claim more likely to have been made by a fantasy fiction author than by a philosophic sect. But think carefully back on what has already been written so far regarding time and the Present Moment. If you have accepted the idea, you will have understood that every material situation involving the human race which exists at this Present Moment – that is, *Now* – is a result of collective positive thoughts, either knowing or involuntary, of the past. Thus the influences of the past have moulded the present, and if not altered, will mould the future. But if, during the next few moments, positive influences are exerted somewhere which alter or cancel out some of the trends of the present, then the potential for the future will immediately be altered. And as the Present Moment is continually decaying into the past, the alteration itself immediately becomes the past. Thus, the past has been altered to adjust the future.

You may consider this merely a play on words (as all Hermetic allegory is), and I accept that it would appear so. Yet, while the conception of Time by the average person remains as it has always been, with the illusion that the past or the future is something concrete, there is no other way to describe it. How much easier to view Time as the old philosophers did, as an eternal Now in which the past, present and future are all one.

Such a view would serve to overcome the misconceptions that have arisen about life after death, and in particular, the subject of reincarnation. It is difficult indeed for the human ego, the personality, to see itself in proper perspective, and in the past it has imagined itself as 'going to heaven' after physical death, there to continue functioning as before. But as Hermetic philosophy has endeavoured to show, the part of the human mind which remains 'immortal', is the 'I', the sense of Being; that part which, for the want of a better term has in the past been called the Soul.

Gnostic literature from all sources will teach this fundamental, and as an example, there is a passage in the Katha-Upanishad, an Indian text, which says:

> The soul is not born; it does not die; it was not produced from anyone. . . . Unborn, eternal, it is not slain, though the body is slain. . . .

This 'I', the great 'I AM' of Exodus, is the Matrix, the collective subconscious, an energy field which in defying our conception of time, records all human life experiences within its sphere of the Present Moment. Thus the personality of the individual, which is not there at birth, but which only develops during the physical life experience, is retained within the Matrix purely as a record of material experience. Upon physical death, the experience stops being recorded. The personality ceases to exist because, the animating spirit being withdrawn, the individual's positive thoughts have ceased. What remains is the subconscious memory record of the whole life experience. It is a feature which induces some unusual phenomena from time to time. Let us take as an instance a story from India, say, which tells of an elderly Guru dying, to be later reincarnated in a baby from another part of the country. When the infant grew old enough to talk, it was found to possess astoundingly detailed knowledge of the Guru's life and circumstances, a phenomenon all the more baffling when it was noted that the child's family had not previously been aware of the Guru's existence. As in the case of the Hexham family mentioned in chapter three, positive thought is the motivating force which induces the phenomenon. The Guru, having reached a successful degree in the art of positive thinking (whatever his own philosophy likes to call it), approaches natural death with the firm belief in reincarnation, and that he will live again in another body. Being impregnated with the Guru's positive thoughts – and, it must be emphasised, the Guru's own conception of reincarnation – the Matrix reacts by implanting in a newly born baby an inlet to the Guru's life experience – not the Guru's personality, or ego, which no longer exists, but his memories. Exactly the same explanation is required to solve the mystery of the Hexham twins.

The same principle also applies in instances of hypnotic regression, except that as no positive thoughts are deliberately being exercised by the regressed subject, the imagination is let loose to play its part. The entranced mind taps into the subconscious memory bank and selects, often at random, a life experience from which the imagination can concoct a convincing and wholly realistic scenario of a 'past life'. As the imagination is creating fiction from factual memory, it is often impossible to determine which parts of the regressive scenario are false and which are truthful.

As with the readings of Edgar Cayce, it is possible for the participants to evoke an intuitional truth within an imaginative scenario, often delivered without warning or apparent reason. In *The Gate of Remembrance*, a volume which annotates Frederick Bligh Bond's efforts to discover through automatic writing, the original extent of the buildings at Glastonbury, much of the communications emanated from a fifteenth century monk named Johannes de Glaston, and in a script which appeared compatible with those times. While the name and some of the information is bound to be a product of the imagination, there is at least one message of some significance to the Hermeticist. On the 4th of December 1915 the initial sequence of automatic writing contained the following:

> . . . The essential facts are eternal which (?move) in a circle, and to them that know the circle, somewhat will pass into all times, only ye see a little at a time. The centre is the point on which all revolve, and ye, revolving, are conscious of the influence, but cannot know the radius. . . .

Discernable within this passage is the principle of the eternal Present Moment.

The author of *Psycho-Cybernetics* raises the subject of subconscious memory storage, reminding readers of an important discovery by the director of the Montreal Neurological Institute, Dr Wilder Penfield. During the course of a brain operation, he happened to touch a small area of the cortex with a surgical instrument. The patient, who as in all such operations, was fully awake, immediately remarked that she was reliving an incident in her childhood which, until that moment, had been consciously forgotten. Similar experiments brought the same reaction. When certain areas of the cortex were touched, the patient did not merely remember past experiences in the usual manner, but *relived* them, all the sights and sounds of the original experience seemingly as real as they once were. While the good doctors express much surprise and astonishment at the way a small component of the human brain can store such a vast amount of information, the Gnostic (Hermeticist) is a lot less surprised.

It has been feared in some quarters that to argue convincingly for Gnosticism against the comfortable, fundamental religious doctrine of the Christian Church might result in a spiritual poverty that would eventually bring chaos. My reply is to point out that chaos and spiritual poverty have been with us for a long time, a poverty of understanding that the Church has done nothing to alleviate.

The power of belief is like a natural water resource – a spring which never dries up. It is there to be used by an opportunist human race which can decide whether to channel it into a clean reservoir, or into a sewer, for as the alchemists have written:

. . . it is found, even in a dung heap. . . .

In a recent survey carried out by a national daily newspaper, several hundred schoolchildren ranging in age from eleven to sixteen, were questioned about their perception of religion and God. In the words of the reporter concerned, a desert of disbelief was uncovered, with little or no support for the established Christian doctrine. God, some protested, was supposed to do fantastic things, but in fact does nothing at all. The conclusion reached by the entire exercise could be aptly summed up by the remarks of one young girl who thought that the whole idea of religion was to believe in something she didn't understand. She even added an erroneous interpretation of John 20, 29 to prove her point:

. . . blessed are they that have not seen and yet have believed.

For this small section of the community – hopefully not representative of the whole – religious or philosophical education is lacking at a time when it is most needed. In centuries gone by, prior to the advent of instantaneous, world wide communication, there was excuse enough for the lack, with many teachers-to-be themselves growing into adulthood within a cocoon of religious ignorance, because the boundaries of their belief were carefully monitored by the Church. Today, it is the end product of this restricted, fundamentalist outlook that has proved to be so lucrative for that wholly American institution, the television evangelist, the collective, exhortive talents of whom had until recently, built the 'God business' into a thriving, billion-dollar-a-year industry. Nationwide disillusionment set in with the advent of 'Pearlygate', when it was discovered that the small screen preachers were all too human, and therefore not as hand in hand with Jesus as many thought them to be.

The one encouraging aspect of the Pearlygate scandal was that many devotees, traumatic over the shattering assault on their cherished beliefs, were induced to seek advice from Fundamentalists Anonymous, an organisation set up in 1985 to rehabilitate those disenchanted with fundamentalism. By 1987, its membership had reached 30,000, but when the TV evangelists disgraced themselves, its resources were overwhelmed, the headquarters in New York besieged by calls from those claiming to have been led into bankruptcy, divorce and suicidal neurosis by the persuasive and highly emotional salesmanship of evangelic programmes.

Pearlygate may well have inflicted a great deal of psychological damage, but it is insignificant compared to the blind stupidity of religious warfare, such as that in Northern Ireland, in the Middle East, and in the conflict between Iran and Iraq, the latter having claimed nearly a million lives. All factions are engaged in deadly combat in support of a figment of the imagination, their religious leaders and themselves as ignorant of the truth as the young schoolgirl mentioned a few paragraphs ago.

In the Middle East, the rapidly rising birthrate of both orthodox Jew (about eight percent of the Israeli population) and Islamic arab, is leading to violent confrontation. Unfortunately for the Israeli Jews, the birthrate of the Palestinian fundamentalist is higher, and supported by Iranian fanatics engaged in the Ayatollah's so-called 'holy' war, demonstrations against the orthodox Jews have become more commonplace and more violent. Both sides have reasons for not wanting to share Palestine, most of which are based on misguided religious beliefs – and if religious fervour runs true to form, both sides will fight it out to the bitter end. Such is the power of Belief.

The problem of the birthrate in Palestine, however, is dwarfed into insignificance by the crisis soon to confront the entire human race – that of over-population on a world wide scale.

In the early days of Homo Sapiens, when his numbers balanced with the rest of animate, animal life, his part in a stable, planetary ecology was akin to a single cog in a well-oiled machine. But that has changed drastically. I need remind no one how over-population is beginning to strain the Earth's natural resources, or how industrial pollution is threatening the planet's whole ecological balance. The life of early Man, if viewed through eyes mesmerized by modern technological wizardry, may appear to have been dull and futile. But haven't we exchanged it for another form of futility? Looking back in time, some might be forgiven for concluding that we were better off as an integral segment of a natural process, than as a dominating force which is destroying everything, including ourselves. The problem of the runaway birthrate exists because of an emotional belief by a humanity that is as hypocritical as it is crass. On the one hand, we do not hesitate to kill millions in religious and political warfare. On the other, we have taken the chance element of survival during infancy out of the hands of Nature, acting out of the very positive belief that all life is 'precious' – all human life, that is, not the rest.

So far, it is the Chinese alone who have taken the only active, nationwide steps towards population control, while in the West, certain religious bodies, to whom a large section of the population look for guidance, refuse to sanction contraception on the grounds that it is against God's purpose – that is, the 'purpose' as seen from their fundamentalist point of view.

The unenviable position in which the human race finds itself today has been brought about by the beliefs of the past, the positive thoughts of our predecessors which have impregnated the Matrix, thus creating our particular Present Moment. It is no wonder that some are prompted to ask the age-old philosophical questions – 'why are we here?', and 'what's it all for?'.

Chapter Nine

One of the most controversial experiments in the early days of electrical research was said to have been performed by a man named Andrew Crosse, a lone experimenter who resided in Somerset. The cause of the controversy was a paper which he wrote and presented to the London Electrical Society in 1837. Therein, he described how he decided to induce the development of artificial crystals by subjecting certain chemicals to prolonged exposure to a weak electrical current. He mixed a solution of silicate or potash and hydrochloric acid into which he placed a lump of oxide of iron. By inducing a low voltage D.C. current to trickle through the solution to the oxide of iron, he hoped to bring about the growth of artificial silicate crystals. He wrote that, on the fourteenth day after the experiment commenced:

> I observed through a small magnifying lens a few small whitish specks clustered around the middle of the electrified stone. Four days later, these specks had doubled in size and had struck out six or eight fine filaments round each speck . . . the filaments were longer than the hemisphere from which they projected. On the 26th day of the experiment, the objects had assumed the form of perfect insects, standing erect on the bristles which they were growing. Although I regarded this as most unusual, I attached no singular significance to it until two days later, the 28th day of the experiment, when the magnifying lens showed that these things were moving their legs. I must say now that I was quite astonished. After a few more days they detached themselves from the stone and moved about through the caustic acid solution.

The paper went on to report that more than a hundred of the tiny creatures were produced. Examination under a microscope revealed that some had six legs, others had eight, and that they were thought to be of the genus *acari*, although others who had seen them believed that they were of an entirely new species. Crosse himself had no idea why they had manifested. He suggested that:

> . . . they must originate in the electrified liquid by some process unknown to me. . . .

Crosse was immediately denounced as a fraud by the leading scientists of the day, to whom his experiment presented a contravention of all accepted belief. Strangely enough, the only champion of Crosse was the chemist, Michael Faraday, who reported that, by following the work as laid down in Crosse's paper, he had also grown the little creatures.

When the furore had died down, Crosse disappeared from public view, leaving his story to remain as an enigma.

Readers of today, in assessing this story, have to decide whether it was true, or a hoax. And therein lies the enigma, for if it was true, why has the experiment not been repeated, giving common access to knowledge of the way in which Man can create insects? Or if it was a hoax, as many believe, why did a scientist of Faraday's stature confirm it?

It is my opinion that the solution to this mystery lies in the ability to recognise Hermetic allegory, which I fully believe this story to be. Referral to the expositions given within the previous two volumes will quickly show that the same necessary code words, or ideas, exist as part of the general theme. Notice, for example, that the experimenter's name is *Crosse* (the philosophic cross, or crucible – in other words, the mind where the development of the understanding takes place). The piece of oxide of *iron* (comparable with the iron nails in the cross) is referred to as the *stone* (the mind), and this stone is placed in an acidic solution (*gall, vinegar*, or the alchemist's *vitriol* – the bitter experience of learning the truth, the recognition that long held beliefs are in error). It is then subjected to a weak, but continuous, electric current (symbol of the *gentle heat* of positive thinking, the effect of which is the *creation of new life*). There is more, but I feel the point is made.

The question arises; why did Faraday support the story? If it is only an allegory, then he could not have duplicated the experiment as he claimed. I would venture that the answer lies in the fact that Faraday himself was fully able to read Hermetic allegory because he was a Hermeticist (positive thinker) himself, in which case he really did duplicate the act of positive thought creation such as the allegory really describes.

It is entirely possible also, that 'Andrew Crosse', whoever he really was, projected the story not simply to draw attention to his own Hermetic understanding, but to emphasise the importance of electrical current as a founding force responsible for the creation of life on this planet, even though his period was well before the time Einstein described all matter as 'congealed electricity'.

The cause of life being created on Earth is a mystery that has occupied the minds of men for centuries, with the answer still seemingly elusive. And yet, a review of up to date knowledge may allow a certain suggestive speculation.

A glance at the most widely accepted theories held by the world's leading authorities will show that our planet is thought to have started its life some 5,000 million years ago as a sphere of molten gas thrown off from the Sun. 1,500 million years later, its rotation had slowed enough for it to solidify and form its rocky outer crust. From this point on, it is the familiar story of life forming in the seas and emerging on to land, the great vegetation of the Palaeozoic setting the scene for the reptillian giants of the Mesozoic Era. The first primates evolved about 14 million years ago, and from them came Man, the late-comer, making an appearance about nine million years BC, but without a brain big enough to warrant the title Human until a mere one million years ago.

Hopefully, this encapsulation of Earth's history is as accurate as collected data will allow, but in truth, the historical accuracy is of secondary importance to the quest. What we really want to know is the reason why, and how, life as we know it formed on Earth alone. We are aware that the wide spectrum of radiation emitted by the Sun promotes growth on our planet, but what of our neighbouring worlds? They bask in the same radiation, and whirl on their orbital paths just as Earth does, yet scientific investigation has revealed that not one of them supports a parallel form of sentient life. Sadly, there are no bug-eyed monsters on Mars, nor little green men on Venus – and the giant outer planets present an infinitely more hostile environment, taxing even the imaginative genius of science fiction writers to conceive some sort of acceptable theory that will accommodate the existence of Jovians, Saturnians, Neptunians and Uranians. Logically, the facts force us to concede that, in our solar system at least, human life is unique to the planet Earth. Thus the prime question; what is it that Earth has got that the others haven't?

Examining the problem from the narrow confines of our own environmental limitations, our first consideration will be the evolutionary period which our planet has reached, it having cooled sufficiently to allow a hot interior to maintain a temperate exterior, thus providing the basic environment necessary to support humans and animals. We have a breathable atmosphere that effectively filters the Sun's radiations, allowing growth-promoting wavelengths to pass and preventing the more lethal rays from harming us. Searching for similar conditions on other planets, and not finding them, we tend to blame their absence for the lack of humanoid species. Yet it has been noticed here on Earth that there are many life forms – animals, insects, and microscopic life – that happily survive in seemingly impossible extremes of temperature, lack of breathable air and other apparently deadly environmental hazards. Because of these discoveries, it has been reluctantly conceded that however hostile the surfaces of other planets may seem, life ought to materialise but for reasons unknown, does not.

Some years ago, biologists discovered a tiny methane producing organism which dates back to Earth's early period and which feeds on a primitive planetary air of hydrogen and carbon dioxide. These ancient organisms are now found only in places where our present atmosphere cannot penetrate, for the oxygen content effectively kills them. From this discovery there emerges the suggestion that, had not something triggered the evolution of the vegetation responsible for the high oxygen content in our atmosphere, the micro-organism and others like it would have gone on contentedly producing methane gas, with the result that our planet's life potential would have been totally different – perhaps the same as the rest. It is discoveries such as this which have forced scientists to re-examine the commonly held theory that animate life on Earth exists solely because of the oxygen-rich atmosphere.

No one can accurately estimate the length of time taken by the Sun in planetary birth. The convulsions that threw off incandescent matter from which the spheres were formed may have been the result of a single, momentous explosion, or there may have been a hundred million years between each ejection. I will not go so far as to say that the time factor is unimportant, but of far more significance is the fact that planetary material all came from the same place and thus each planet is composed of the same basic elements and therefore ought to hold the same potential for the production of animate life forms. But obviously, something is lacking in all the other planets. No one planet is like another as regards mass, speed of orbit and distance from the Sun. With the greatest of confidence we can assume that the giant outer planets are the farthest removed from Earth in terms of compatible environmental conditions and so it is logical to turn to our near neighbours, the planets of relatively similar size, in search of comparable biological status.

We may at once dispose of Mercury, for this innermost sphere, only two fifths the size of Earth and heavily influenced by the Sun's gravitational field, has slowed to a degree where all atmosphere, if there ever had been any, has long since dispersed. It is a rocky, barren world where the surface temperature is hot enough to melt zinc – about 400 degrees centigrade.

Venus, on the other hand, is the same size and mass as Earth, with a similar surface gravity, and for a long time astronomers felt that its dense covering of cloud could well have concealed a world comparable to the earlier stages of terrestrial life. This conjecture led many writers to envision a prehistoric hothouse of Venusian dinosaurs and giant rain forests. But recent space probes have radioed back disappointing data. The Green Planet is heavily shrouded in an atmosphere that consists mainly of carbon dioxide, and a barometer on the surface would register a pressure of more than nine times that of Earth. The surface temperature is not much less than that of Mercury and is maintained day and night. If it rains at all, the clouds deposit sulphuric acid, not water. No one can envisage what the planet's surface looks like, but there are certainly no carpets of forest or vegetation. Finally, Venus lacks one thing which may be vital to the production of humanoid life – it has no magnetic field.

Mars, our nearest outward neighbour, was at one time the centre of much hopeful speculation in the search for sentient life. It seemed a better proposition altogether, despite the fact that it orbits the Sun fifty million miles further out than Earth, for there were signs of polar caps that changed with the seasons and a colouring that looked very much as if it were a form of vegetation. With the historic visit by the Viking Space Probe, however, our hopes were once again dashed. It was found that the Red Planet does have an atmosphere of a kind, although it too consists mainly of carbon dioxide, with very little oxygen, and very much thinner than our own. Regardless of the fact that the polar caps are indeed snow and that some water vapour is present on the planet, the necessary evolution of organic life into the higher forms has not taken place. The surface temperature appears inhospitable, being a mere ten degrees centigrade at its warmest, while at night dropping to minus eighty, but we know from the existence of life forms on our own planet that these Arctic conditions are not in themselves enough to preclude the possibility of life. The equatorial belt on Mars suffers some dust storms and there is a certain amount of volcanic action. In short, the planet offers an environment very much like a cold, dry Earth. Yet we search in vain for the slightest sign of a long-departed race of Martians. Although there are still many arguments to be settled over the implications of the experiments performed by the Viking Probe while on Martian soil, there are certain aspects of the data which offer a slender, speculative clue as to the reason why no such higher evolutionary life exists there.

From the scoops of Martian soil secured by the robot arm of the Probe, it was found that although certain organisms were present and could be made to metabolise in the artificially induced environment of the test chamber, *they would not reproduce.* Further, a sample of Californian soil, carried to Mars in the Probe and subjected to the same test while on the alien planet, showed the same result. Whereas they would reproduce in test conditions at home, they would not do so on Mars. Of the possible answers to this minor mystery, one is that there exists some element on Earth which is not present on Mars, and which is vital to the act of reproduction.

No scientific genius is required to name the prime element associated with reproduction on planet Earth. It is the moon.

The lunar rhythm is, of course, only one of many cyclic influences under which we all live, but it is by far the strongest. Generations of farmers and fishermen have timed their work according to the phases of the moon, acting on traditional knowledge handed down from antiquity. Latter-day research with sophisticated equipment spawned by the electronic age has served only to confirm the old superstitions, much to the amazement of the technicians involved. Their instruments have even detected heat emanating from the moon's surface. It cannot be felt, but it has been measured.

Apart from its effect on plant, animal and oceanic life, we are now very much aware that the lunar influence can be responsible for earth tremors when its tidal action overstresses the crust of the Earth. The weather, too, comes under the orb's dictates, for the tidal influence is present in the atmosphere, causing changes to barometric pressure. So all-pervading is its effect that it will produce a miniature tide in something as small as a teacup full of liquid – and when it is remembered that the human brain is eighty percent water, it will be apparent that the moon's influence over human behaviour might be more than just a myth. Study of recent years has shown mounting evidence of the dominating lunar effect on blood flow, patterns of violence, and most important of all, the reproductive cycle of the female.

Early Man was intuitively aware of this, and collective archaeological findings show that his interest in the bright Queen of the Night was obsessive. Science writer, Alexander Marshack, after an exhaustive study of all available published material and artifacts of the Upper Palaeolithic Era, plus a first hand examination of caves, reached the conclusion that as far back as 30,000 BC, men were carefully noting the 29 to 30 day cycle of the Moon. The gargantuan stone monoliths of the Neolithic Era bear witness to the fact that this avid interest did not stop at a few scratches on a shard of bone, or on the wall of a cave, but manifested in the construction of some of the world's most impressive monuments. The vast array of standing stones at Carnac, in Brittany, and our own Stonehenge, to name but two, were erected with one prime purpose in view – to compute the exact position of the moon on any given day of the year. All over the globe, various cultures have been found to possess a common foundation of legend and tradition surrounding the moon, with many such beliefs prevailing even in the hard-fact atmosphere of the twentieth century.

Earth, at some remote period in its evolution, captured the moon. Just when is impossible to determine, but technical estimates range from 600,000 years ago to as far back as two thousand million. Lunar rocks brought back by the Apollo missions have been subjected to the most accurate dating systems available and have been found to be an incredible four and a half billion years old. This evaluation does not mean that the moon was established in orbit round the Earth for all that length of time, it merely gives some idea of the satellite's antiquity.

Age readings of lunar rocks have presented scientists with something of an enigma, for one report, published in America's *Science News*, June 1973 edition, revealed that one moon rock had been dated at 5.3 billion years. This was a considerable shock to researchers, for the oldest known rocks on Earth are only 3.7 billion years of age. It was a piece of information that upset a number of fondly cherished theories, but the most chagrined were those who subscribed to the idea that the moon was once a part of Earth, and that the two had separated in the early stages of planetary evolution. Our knowledge of celestial mechanics prior to the lunar landings had already relegated this hypothesis to the realm of the improbable, but the hoary antiquity of the rock datings finished the argument altogether. That left two major propositions, namely the Sister Planet, and the Capture Theory. The former idea, that the moon was a twin of Earth, formed at the same time, received a fair amount of scientific support at first, but information gleaned from the Apollo data, underlining the difference in planetary make-up between the two bodies, cast too much doubt for the theory to remain tenable. The last, and the most likely explanation, is that the moon was a wandering asteroid, probably an early ejection from the Sun which fell into a comet-like orbit across the span of the solar system and which eventually was attracted to and captured by the Earth's gravitational field. But even this theory doesn't satisfy all, for some maintain that the Moon's orbit is its one best argument against gravitational capture, because its path is too neat. Had it been pulled into captivity it should have settled into a more eccentric path than it now follows. Some extreme theorists go so far as to state that, had the moon come from outside Earth's planetary field, it would have required to have been *steered* into its present orbit, that it would never have fallen into it by chance. This speculation was enough to arouse the imagination of certain writers who suggested that the satellite had been engineered into position by a race of super-technological beings, who were even now observing us from their UFOs. To what end was not specified!

The facts may yield a less sensational answer. Certainly the path of the moon's orbit is unusual, but there is nothing about it that cannot be explained in the light of the data obtained from the Apollo missions. The answer lies in the fact that the moon's surface has some extremely unusual properties, and it is these, combined in interaction with the Earth's own magnetic field, that has brought the satellite into its present position.

On a clear night when the moon is full, gaze up at the shining orb and you will see those familiar dark patches which form the 'face'. Early astronomers thought that these were great oceans similar to our own, accordingly naming them Marias, the Latin name for seas. The two patches that make up the eyes are the Mare Imbrium and the Mare Tranquillitatis – and it takes no great stretch of one's imagination to appreciate that some of these areas are immense. The Oceanus Procellarus, for instance, covers a vast two million square miles. Intense scientific interest was centred on these areas when it was found that some of the Apollo spacecraft, when passing directly over the Marias, registered a downward pull and a slight acceleration. Every lunar probe directed to fly over the Maria reacted in the same way and technicians could only draw the obvious conclusion that the gravitational pull exerted by these areas was stronger than at other parts of the lunar surface. Evaluation of data brought back by the landing parties led to the discovery that the areas were actually vast deposits of mineral ore. This high concentration resulted in a correspondingly heavier mass, which in turn was responsible for the increased gravitational pull. To put it simply, the areas acted as vast, giant magnets. Applying their own inimitable jargon, the scientists labelled these areas 'mascons', short for mass concentrations. Another inexplicable facet of lunar mystery was encountered when technicians were able to examine the first photographs of the dark side of the moon. It is common knowledge that the satellite has no axial spin other than the single revolution which takes place over the period in which it orbits Earth. Therefore the same lunar face is always presented to the earthbound observer. The question as to what was on the other side has always been under speculation, and when the Russians' space flight brought back the first pictures, scientists all over the world were eager to examine them. They were astonished to find that the dark side is radically different from the familiar face. While far more pock-marked with giant craters and criss-crossed with magnificent mountain ranges, it has strangely few Maria. Everyone agreed that the largest areas of mascons were to be found on the face that is always shown to Earth – and here lies the explanation for the moon's lack of axial spin and the irregularity of its orbit which has so perturbed certain scientists.

Almost every other planetary satellite in the solar system has been noted to circle its respective parent orb in the plane of the planet's equator, but our moon's orbit lies outside the equatorial path, yawing first to one side and then the other in cyclic eccentricity. Speculating on the reason for this, it may be suggested that when the moon was captured by Earth's magnetic field, the interaction between this field and the gravitational pull exerted by the one-sided disposition of the moon's mascons areas, pulled the satellite into its wobbly path, and then served to slow its axial spin until the face containing the most mascons was held in firm attraction towards Earth.

This, in itself, is a one in a million event in celestial

mechanics, but there exists a further vital factor that was to enhance the moon's properties a billionfold.

The moon's diameter of 2,160 miles does not qualify it for the title of the solar system's largest satellite, for there are the moons Titan and Triton, the biggest of those which circle Saturn and Neptune respectively. There is also Ganymede, the largest satellite of Jupiter. All three are bigger than Luna, but the parent bodies of this trio are the massive, outer planets, the smallest of which has a diameter of 27,000 miles compared to Earth's modest 8,000. What is wholly unique, therefore, is the fact that no other satellite in the system is quite so large in relation to its parent body, *or exerts quite so much magnetic influence on it*, for our moon is a monstrous one fourth the size of Earth.

The Apollo data brought to light one other remarkable and hitherto unsuspected fact about the lunar orb – that it has a strange, out of round bulge.

Admittedly, it is unlikely that any planetary body has a perfectly spherical shape due to the action of gravitational force. Even the Earth bulges out at the Equator and is therefore slightly larger in diameter there than at the poles. But the moon has a most unusual bulge outwards on its far side, the face we never see. The difference in this out-of-round is about .06 percent, which means that the surface of the far side sticks up some three miles higher than it should, whilst the familiar face is correspondingly lower. A relatively insignificant figure, you may think, when measured against a total diameter of more than two thousand miles, but the internal stresses suggested by this irregularity would be tremendous.

At first, scientists attributed the bulge to the great power of Earth's gravitational pull, but other data rendered this conclusion unlikely, for the effect is seventeen times greater than it should be if caused by tidal influence, and it would be expected that the bulge be facing Earth, not the opposite. Careful consideration will reveal that the most unusual properties of the high mascon areas are responsible for the enigma. The one-sided placement of the areas, formed as they were before capture by the Earth and when the satellite was in the process of 'setting', caused the heavily concentrated face to be pulled towards its own centre of gravity, whilst the opposite, forced by axial spin, bulged outwards in counteraction. When the whole sphere hardened and was captured by Earth's magnetic field, the satellite naturally settled into its present position, the giant magnets of the mascons pointing towards Earth, leaving the outer bulge locked in position on the hidden side.

In considering the implications of this situation, it may help to examine an elementary form of dynamo such as that used to light the lamps of a pedal cycle. Take one to pieces and you will discover that it consists only of a cylindrical magnet which is positioned to revolve at high speed within a coil which is wrapped around a metal frame. The simple action of the inner magnet revolving inside the coiled wire produces a magnetic flux, making a second magnet out of the metal frame and producing electricity in the wires of the coil. Now picture the Earth and the moon as two magnets – for that is precisely what they are. In planetary terms, the moon is revolving round the Earth at high speed, in close proximity and following a cyclic path – an oscillation – which causes a magnetic flux, just as in the dynamo. Would it be unreasonable to expect some reaction to this production of energy?

We may speculate that the reason why Venus carries no comparable life form does not rest with the surface conditions alone, but because it has no magnetic field with which to capture a satellite. Mars, although possessing a magnetic field, has managed to secure only two asteroids of insignificant size, the largest being a mere thirteen miles across and with no qualities comparable to the moon. The influence of both, therefore, is negligible. Earth's relationship with the moon seems to be a freak of celestial mechanics, for the same situation is not to be found elsewhere.

Biologists agree that life as we know it began in the oceans, and it is these great bodies of water which are most affected by the lunar influence. In the far past, after the moon had been captured and its axial spin was halted, the full force of the mascons, twice the gravitational pull of the Sun, triggered a unique reaction by stimulating the reproduction of minute organisms which evolved into seaweed and other oceanic life.

As the great stewpot of the oceans was stirred by the lunar ladle, and as the eccentricity of the moon's orbit produced the cyclic phenomenon of alternating high and low tides, life was washed up on the shore, not to be reclaimed by the sea at the next, and lower, tide. Thus a gradual advance on to land took place, with sea life adapting itself to conditions on land, a dramatic generation which culminated in the great forested areas that covered our planet in prehistoric times. Because of this, the atmosphere became oxygen-enriched, dictating that animate life should be oxygen breathers.

As each and every life form evolved, including the eventual arrival of Man, it did so under the dominating influence of the moon's magnetic cycle. Thus, we may be forced to accept that, as far as the solar system is concerned, Man is the result of an accidental celestial whim – the chance capture of a strange shaped asteroid by the third planet from the Sun. It is a proposition which may not be welcomed by those who believe that there exists a Creator with a Grand Design in which the human race is playing an important and prominent part.

It is also a proposition which may explain why the older philosophers maintained that the moon was 'evil', an un-accountable edict usually interpreted in relation to the well known effects exerted on certain unstable individuals at the time of a full moon. But the explanation goes far deeper than that. The moon, as the fundamental cause of human existence on Earth, is seen as the influence which spawned the conscious mind of Man. It is the attraction of the senses which draws the 'immaculate' power of the collective subconscious during each lifetime, holding it a prisoner within the physical body. Thus, the moon was held to be responsible for the 'fall' of the 'immaculate', or 'perfect' material into the degradation of physical matter. In regard to mankind's current aspirations in the sphere of spatial exploration, we may consider the possibility of a parallel humanoid life form existing on a planet belonging to some distant star, conceding that such an event is possible. Somewhere, perhaps, in the awesome, almost inconceivable remoteness of inter-galactic space, there may well have been a duplication of the freak circumstances which culminated in the advent of Man, but I leave it to the reader to calculate the probability of the two cultures ever meeting in the flesh.

It is the imagination, of course, which has given us Captain Kirk of the starship Enterprise, using a warp drive to bridge the vast distances of interstellar space, and to date, only the imagination can supply an answer to the crucial question of how matter, in the shape of human flesh, can be made to travel at the speed of light, let alone to exceed it, as would be necessary for such journeys. If, however, science should confirm that the old philosophers were correct, and that the moon is indeed the essential power behind our reproductive system, then the advance of mankind beyond the sphere of that influence would be limited to one generation, for there would be no new births en route to the next star system.

Another major factor requiring consideration is the proposition that human life has evolved as it has by means of its own positive thinking, the subconscious needs of each species determining the form into which it evolves. Thus, not only must mankind bridge space and find a planet with identical environmental conditions, he must also search for a species of humanoids with the same subconscious, evolutionary inclinations.

Astute readers will immediately argue that if the positive thoughts of Jules Verne were responsible for a successful flight to the moon and back, then the same positive thinking ought to take us to the stars. I reply that the trip to the moon was, in comparable terms, like an ant covering the first quarter of an inch of what others are hoping will be a walk round the world. The mathematical equations which confirm the postulates put forward by Albert Einstein in his theory of Relativity, show indisputably that the constant known as the 'speed of light' is a limit at which matter ceases to be, and therefore precludes human flesh from ever attaining it.

This constant, however, has much significance for the Hermeticist in that, from the human point of view, it is both *formless* and *timeless* – as is the Present Moment.

Chapter Ten

It was Albert Einstein who remarked that 'common sense' is in fact nothing more than a deposit of prejudices laid down in the mind prior to the age of eighteen, and that every new idea encountered thereafter is forced to fight against this accretion of 'self-evident' concepts. Self analysis will quickly show that he was right. In their formative years, children imitate their elders. Their empty memory banks are receptacles not solely for ideas, opinions and conclusions resulting from their own initial experiences, but also for habits, customs, superstitions, dogma, philosophy and ethics taught to them by parents and other elders around them. Once these beliefs are firmly entrenched within the young mind, their influences may endure for a lifetime unless the subject is either fortunate enough to experience a revelation, or far-seeing enough to begin analysis of himself. It is the latter which the *Confessio*, the second of the Rosicrucian Manifestos, urged everyone to embark upon:

> . . . the which perhaps would not be so hard to do as if one should begin to pull down and destroy the old ruinous building, and then enlarge the forecourt, afterwards bring lights in the lodgings, and then change the doors, stairs, and other things according to our intention. . . .

It is self-analysis, the demolition of the 'old ruinous building' that prior to enlightenment, brings the 'suffering', the *nigredo* stage of the process, during which the neophyte experiences the acid touch of the alchemist's *vitriol*. As Carl Jung put it,

> It is bitter indeed to discover behind one's lofty ideals narrow, fanatical convictions, all the more cherished for that, and behind one's heroic pretensions nothing but crude egotism, infantile greed, and complacency.

Ultimately, before anyone can aspire to a successful

manipulation, *consciously*, of the Matrix in order to beneficially influence their own destiny, all prejudice must be expunged and a total understanding of the Belief principle acquired. And it must be added that while advice to embark upon such a course can be freely given, the work cannot be forced upon the individual, nor can it be completely taught. The *distillation* takes place in the *retort*, or *vase* – that is, in the alchemist's own mind as he, or she, experiments upon Self. In other words, the true positive thinker will acquire use of the power only by individual effort.

As every human action takes place as a result of the Belief principle at work, external evidence of it is always to hand. Why, for instance, do we celebrate the annual event known as All Fools' Day, in which the morning is spent trying to make others believe something that is not true? The alchemist of old would enlighten you by saying that everyone was *playing with the First Matter* – and thus it requires no effort of deduction to realise that the event is a Gnostic joke against the Church, inaugurated by some amused positive thinker of the past. While external effects such as this are quickly recognised, to define the cause, or source, of the Belief principle within one's own mind is a lot less easy. Clearly, many have found that just to sit down and read through *The Power Of Positive Thinking* is not enough to bring success. The neophyte may find some salvation in a study of hypnotic practice, for it is during hypnosis that the subject's reasoning power, which includes the ability to doubt, is muted. The hypnotised mind is more open to suggestion that the waking mind – which is another way of stating that the hypnotised mind is more ready to *believe* than when awake. And as with positive thinking, the subconscious responds when the belief is strong enough and not hindered by doubt.

In one medical experiment, a dermatologist named Kreibich hypnotised a colleague and then touched his skin with a matchstick, at the same time suggesting that he had been burned. The subject was immediately brought out of his trance, and a few minutes later that spot that had been touched became inflamed. In a few more minutes, the skin had raised into a blister. The next day, the blister was removed for examination and it was found that the tissue changes which had taken place were identical to those of a real burn. The comparison with the manifestation of stigmata is irresistible, and indeed, has been made by medical men themselves. The inescapable conclusion is that the inner mind has unlimited power over the structure of matter. As Isaac Newton widened the horizons of his understanding of gravitation through unceasing study and by dwelling constantly on the subject, so the neophyte may probe the deeper mysteries of positive thinking by a careful study of the works named in this book, reading them not merely the once, but time and again until more than just a superficial comprehension is achieved.

Emile Coué, for example, makes a vitally important point when he emphasises the difference between positive thinking and wishful thinking, both of which are motivated by desire, although each in a different way. It is wishful thinking which will conflict with the subconscious, the reason resting with the intricacies of Time perception. Coué warns that it would be wrong to phrase an auto-suggestion with the words; 'I will make this happen.' Rather, he advises, you should say, 'this thing is coming to pass'. The former statement raises difficulties on two counts, firstly because it is phrased in the future tense – 'I will make this happen' (a promise, the happening not yet achieved), as opposed to 'I am making this happen' (present tense), or 'I have made this happen' (past tense). Placed in the future tense, it immediately comes into conflict with the present tense of the subconscious, the Present Moment. Secondly, by use of the personal dictate, 'I will', the conscious mind's own will is invoked, which the subconscious may resist. But if the desire is presented to the subconscious with the phrase; 'this thing is coming to pass', there is no invocation of the personal will. Instead, it is a simple statement in the present tense, by an observer, of a positive act of creation. Hence, the subconscious will find it acceptable, and will oblige. All those who have been diligent enough to have studied the older manuscripts themselves will have encountered the advice to 'become an observer'. This is an example of what it means.

The objection might be raised: does not this analysis conflict with Coué's injunction to say, 'Every day, in every way, *I am* getting better and better', for with the use of 'I', the personal ego is invoked? The answer is that there is no conflict because the statement is an observation, not a dictate, although its successful application will depend upon your belief in it. As an observation of something that is happening now (at the Present Moment), the accompanying feeling must be one of unquestioned Belief in the outcome, but if the belief is half-hearted then Desire may colour it, invoked by the *hope* that it will come true. If this is the case, the suggestions will certainly fail.

The importance of feeling is stressed by Helen Rhodes Wallace, in *How To Enter The Silence*, when she writes

> The mind is not capable of bringing anything to pass except it be accompanied by the emotional counterpart of the idea.

Al Koran, in *Bring Out The Magic In Your Mind*, is just as adamant regarding this point:

> Feeling is the secret. You obtain your desire by feeling as if you had already got what you want. . . .

In the act of *knowing*, your belief in a specific objective will be reinforced if you can conjure up within your mind the emotions which you would experience if the event were already a reality. If you wish to be rich, then *feel* rich.

In 1984, a national daily newspaper covered the activities of American Jerry Gillies, who charges £3,500 a seminar for teaching what he calls Prosperity Consciousness. He believes that no matter what they say outwardly, people have a resistance to the idea of being rich, an inner feeling that they have not earned it, an attitude engendered by the Protestant work ethic. But that can be changed.

> There is a certain air about someone who thinks they're worth a lot. It seems almost magical, but I know when I feel a certain way about myself that people just appear offering me money.

Al Koran, who is equally explicit on the subject of prosperity, says that

> If you are poor, it is your own fault. You had to see yourself poor, had to think of yourself as being poor, or you would never have been poor. You had to speak of poverty or you would never have been empty-handed. The subconscious creates what you give it.

Koran informs readers that the interpretation of the word 'meditation' is the act of being mindful, attentive and aware of the picture you wish to create. Speak to your subconscious self every day, commanding money, knowing that it will come. Ask constantly and at the same time feel so glad that it is coming that you can hardly contain your joy. He insists that

> There is no lack in the world. The lack is in you.

It is Al Koran's text that reveals a particular aspect of Hermetic symbolism, that of 'temptation', which figures so prominently in the story of Rennes le Chateau. The Roman Catholic Church portrays Satan as some kind of invisible devil, or influence which tempts one into sin, meaning any act which violates the accepted moral code. The real meaning is a lot less of an abstraction.

If you are attempting to think yourself positively into wealth, and you catch sight of your empty wallet, this – according to Koran – is the tempter, for it is tempting you to see *double*. The sight of the wallet, the realisation that it is empty, may cause Doubt to enter your thinking, whereas only Certainty should be there if success is to be achieved. Al Koran's analysis is perfectly correct. The so-called 'original sin' of the Bible is the act of Doubting. Granted that to imagine yourself rich when there is a shortage of money, to feel no desire for cash when there is need of it, requires you to adopt a deliberately schooled frame of mind out of which it is easy to slip, and which cannot be accomplished in a day or two, no matter how hard you try. There is always a lapse into a feeling of wanting, often before you become conscious of it. To fight that mental fight requires dedication, time and patience. That is why Alchemy (positive thinking) was called an Art, and why its results were collectively called the Gift of God.

The complexity of Austin Osmand Spare's literary style means that considerable interpretive skill is needed to extract the undoubtedly valuable information that it offers. In *The Book of Pleasure*, the attributes of the conscious and the subconscious minds are called ZOS and KIA respectively, while he introduces such phrases as 'the death posture' and 'the neither-neither' in an effort to portray in words states of mind that are abstract. Much of the text deals with the qualities of Belief and its connection with Will and Desire, upon which the reader is asked to meditate. Will and Belief should be conceived as a unity, he maintains.

> Existing as dual, they are identical in desire; by their duality there is no control, for will and belief are ever at variance. . . . Let him unite them.

He points out that a certain 'vacuity' of mind should be attained, but warns that this is not to be gained, as others have taught, by focussing the mind on a 'negation of all conceivable things', but by perceiving and feeling without the necessity of an opposite. As you can immediately see, the fundamentals expressed here is of a choice between Certainty and Doubt.

The subject of mental vacuity provides an opportunity to correct some false impressions which have been encouraged by those who advocate 'transcendental meditation'. Following the dictates of ill-informed, self-styled 'adepts' in India, they have spread the notion that it is necessary to stop all thought in order to reach the subconscious – and while this is fundamentally true, it is not a literal truth. As John G. Bennet has stated, as long as one attempts to keep an image out of one's thoughts, it constantly recurs.

> Thus all that commonly passes for 'meditation' and 'concentration' is a form of exclusion and is really negative.
>
> (*The Path of Subub – 1958*)

The real capacity to still thought, to which everything in Hermeticism is related, lies in the ability to monitor and eventually discard all negative emotions and prejudices. Aldous Huxley, in *The Perennial Philosophy*, quotes the philosopher Molinos as distinguishing three degrees of silence; silence of the mouth, of the mind, and of the will.

Huxley goes on to say:

> To refrain from idle talk is hard; to quiet the gibbering
> memory and imagination is much harder. Hardest of all
> is to still the voices of craving and aversion within the
> will.

Whereas the Indian mystics tell their neophytes to 'stop
thought', Helen Rhodes Wallace advocates an entering into
the silence which, as we have previously discovered, to her
means the silencing of

> . . . all unreality, of doubt, fear, false belief, worry,
> complaining, grief, of everything that is merely of the
> outer personality. . . .

Spare, with his 'vacuity', 'death-posture', and 'neither-
neither', is referring to the same state of mind. However, there
is a particular aspect of the 'stopping thought' concept,
generally overlooked, upon which we have not so far touched,
and from which the current misconceptions may well have
evolved.

An essential part of Spare's method by which he implanted a
desire in the subconscious, was called 'union through
absent-mindedness'. This is a technique of deliberately
forgetting the desire during its period of 'magical invocation'.
For the operation to succeed, for the desire to successfully
materialise, the conscious mind must play no part once it has
imagined the desire (made its wish). If it does, then it
immediately projects more of the desire, which is of course
counterproductive in effect. The most propitious time, Spare
says, to despatch a desire to the subconscious is when the mind
is in a state of *vacuity*, a state which is achieved every now and
again when a flow of thought runs its course and is exhausted.
Before commencing thought upon some other subject, there
is a brief instant of pause by the mind, which is seldom, if ever,
noticed. This pause, Spare says, is true vacuity.

From this description it might appear to be well nigh
impossible a task to succeed in catching a pause that is so quick
that it is hardly noticeable, but think carefully about it. If the
state of vacuity occurs at the end of a train of thought, all that is

necessary is to institute a train of thought related to the desire. Then, when a new train of thought begins, great care must be taken not to recall the original train of thought to mind, for it would destroy the implantation in the subconscious. As we have already seen, the reason why the implantation would be destroyed is because – assuming the neophyte is properly considering the desire as *already come true* – the recall would superimpose a future tense over it, thus nullifying the positive effect.

In his own peculiar and obscure way, Spare reiterated this by resorting to the oldest known form of Hermetic allegory with which to describe the conscious and the subconscious minds – the penis and the womb respectively. He describes how an urn must be constructed, an 'earthenware virgin', in conformity to the dimensions of the erect penis. Sufficient space was to be provided at the bottom of the urn's cavity so that a vacuum would form when the phallus was inserted. The cavity was to contain the desire, which would be automatically consecrated at the moment of orgasm. At this critical moment, the desire was to be held vividly in mind for as long as possible. When it began to wane and disappear, the urn was to be hermetically sealed and buried in a casket filled with earth, or in the ground itself. Spare described the Earthenware Virgin as

> . . . the most formidable formula known; it never fails and is dangerous. Hence what is not written down must be guessed.

The 'urn' is, of course, the mind, the womb of the subconscious into which the desire must be injected. The 'moment of orgasm' is the pause at the end of the train of desiring thought, and the 'burial' represents the forgetting of the desire once it has been thus projected. And isn't the 'vacuum' mentioned reminiscent of Eliphas Levi's instructions?

The Book Of Pleasure is best known for its exposition of Spare's process of 'sigilization', a means whereby a specific desire may be implanted in the subconscious. As an example, the author gives I DESIRE THE STRENGTH OF A TIGER. To make a sigil of this, all the letters are written down, omitting repetitions. The remainder are then combined in the form of a single glyph which, when seen by the eye, will be immediately recognised by the subconscious as representative of the desire. Once sigilized in this manner, Spare says, the desire itself must be completely forgotten.

No doubt many have tried to put this process into practice and have been disappointed to find that it does not work, and it must again be emphasised that the principle in question here is one of belief. To sigilize a desire in this fashion could be construed as a form of positive thinking, and if every aspect of the Hermetic process is followed, then there is no reason for it not to be successful. But success does not rest in the fact of sigilization. May I remind readers of the words of Paracelsus, who stated quite unequivocally that

> The exercise of true magic does not require any ceremonies or conjurations or the making of circles, or signs; it requires neither benedictions nor maledictions in words, neither verbal blessings or curses; it only requires a strong faith in the omnipotent power of all good, that can accomplish everything if it acts through a human mind who is in harmony with it. . . .

Thus we are quite clearly instructed that although we may think we need an external ritual to focus our consciousness, it is never the ritual which works the miracle, but the strength of *faith* exercised by the mind. If there is no faith, all the ritual in the world would be useless.

If all thoughts of out-of-the-body phenomena as popularly understood can be set to one side, the text of *Practical Astral Projection* presents similarly invaluable advice and information for the would-be positive thinker. The 'projection' of the title is in fact the projection of the mind into a sphere of positive Certainty. But, Yram warns, before attainment of that state, there are some *sacrifices* to be made on the part of the candidate.

It must be remembered that every time one thinks, an energy roughly comparable to electricity is brought into play. In obedience to the fundamental law 'like attracts like', the character of your thoughts will infallibly reciprocate on yourself. Therefore, if you live a life of personal desirelessness, without self-centred aims, acting in a detached manner for the general usefulness of the community around you, there will be a gradual disengagement from the downward energy expressing matter, accompanied by a deepening of the understanding of the powers of Nature. But if your thoughts are only of yourself, motivated by greed and personal profit, the magnetic thought-field thus formed will attract energies of a similar quality, the very nature of which will force you to experience the same type of attractions over and over again.

> For you it is easier to give way to these attractions than to create new ones. To destroy them means real suffering. We all know the power of habit and the sweetness of obeying its call. Having no better reason for changing your mode of existence you go on living this way your whole life through.

Even Al Koran, who in a wholly material vein advises readers to demand money from the subconscious as the way to acquire material wealth, agrees with this point, saying:

> Whatever you want, you have only to make up your mind and work within the law . . . the first law of business is 'give and take'. But you must give before you can take. . . .

Great consideration must be given to that last sentence. Failure to observe this point is the reason why so many are never successful in the art of positive thinking.

When the older manuscripts advise readers to think inwardly and to become conscious of Self, being positive in your outlook, it does not mean that you must adopt an attitude of aggressive, egotistical self-aggrandizement. Equally, when personal desirelessness is advocated, it does not imply that there should be no ambition. To lie, fear, cheat, hate and be jealous of others are immature emotions, expressed by those trapped in evolutionary infancy. All that is required to break free is the exercise of positive moral purity. Yram declares that morality is an intelligent selection of the forces favourable to one's evolution, adding that such volution is imposed by the active composition of both man and universe. It is by correct moral conduct alone that the adept may synchronise both worlds. The benefits of a successful

Hermetic process, according to Yram, is an ultimate possession of a consciousness that is a unity with the principle of the subconscious, a universal order. Once achieved, it is impossible for the adept to conceive a better system for the simple reason that, having reached the Absolute, a more perfect state does not exist. Good and evil no longer hold their former significance, and to continue to attribute meaning to them would be an error of judgement. This is not possible for an adept, for once in union with Nature, there is bestowed upon the conscious mind a 'kind of perfect intuition', which allows full realisation of thee universality of its power an range of action.

> By instinct, he feels that at the least desire, at the most feeble attraction, at the very shade of thought, the whole of his psychological faculties will set to work as one. At one and the same instant he has weighed, meditated on, and acted without the collective whole of his functions hindering in the least his confident serenity, indicative of universal wisdom.

Yram lays out three conditions for success in development of perfect adeptship. The first of these requires the novice to have *confidence*. Secondly, *goodwill* towards others, so that the novice himself can lead a tranquil existence. Finally, he is required to *think unceasingly of the result to be obtained*.

Conclusion

It is an essential facet of human nature that, sooner or later in life, there will be experienced an inner urge, a spiritual yearning, a need to formulate a personal philosophy by which material existence can be measured and, hopefully, justified. Shallow thinkers will parasitize the beliefs of others, often ignorant and indifferent to the fact that there is no solid foundation of truth to uphold the particular credo they have selected. The more intuitive choose to think with their own minds rather than allow others to think for them, and in the end, it is these who are attracted to Gnosticism. They gravitate towards it, not due to the influence of advertisement or exhortation, but because of an unfolding process on the mind conducted by Nature itself.

Gnosticism, Rosicrucianism, Hermeticism, by whatever signature the doctrine may be found represented, is no figment of the imagination. Although concealed, it has been the property of mankind since the dawn of intelligence, detectable as the true foundation of all so-called 'pagan' religions, and already a philosophy of hoary antiquity by the time Catholicism introduced its tenets of Christianity.

As the adepts themselves have repeatedly stated, Gnosis can be learned but it cannot be taught, and therefore this book with its two companion volumes, does not pretend to be an explicit manual whereby the novice can read and gain immediate access to magical powers. Neither is it an appeal for converts, for such an appeal, if made at all, is the prerogative of Nature. This trilogy merely indicates a door – you open it yourself, but only if you wish to do so. If you are already satisfied with whatever religious code you live under, be it Mohammedism, Islamism, Buddhism, Christianity or even Atheism, then remain so until the dictates of that inner need are personally experienced. When that occurs, the development of the understanding – the *golden understanding* –

becomes possible as a free choice of the individual, and the principle of positive thinking, as it is appreciated by the public at large, can be seen as merely a minor part of a much greater possibility.

Appendix

The Turin Shroud:
The recent revelation by scientists involved in subjecting fragments of the Shroud of Turin to carbon dating analysis requires some comment here in view of my remarks concerning it in chapter thirteen of *Hermes Unveiled*. Therein, I referred readers firstly to a conjecture put forward by Ian Wilson, in his admirable work, *The Turin Shroud*, (1978) – namely that the earlier Mandylion, the image 'not made with human hands', and the Shroud should be considered as one and the same. Secondly, I contended that the image on the Shroud (and of the Mandylion) was placed there by what the lay person would call 'supernatural' means, as the result of a strong mental force acting upon the matter of the cloth at atomic level so as to produce the picture which has been the subject of so much controversy.

Some may be of the opinion that the revelation of the Shroud's age, the results showing that it originated somewhere between 1,000 and 1,500 AD, will have served to invalidate everything I wrote concerning both the Mandylion and the Shroud. With respect, I beg to differ, and now offer the reasons why.

May I immediately remind readers that the major reaction to the carbon dating result emerged as a great cry of 'fake!'. Yes . . . but of course, it is only a 'fake' to those masses entrapped by religious teaching into believing that Jesus Christ was actually a living entity who suffered crucifixion in the manner described in the Gospels. The Fundamentalists, therefore, are the real casualties of the revelation. Since Church doctrine is immovably dogmatic in this belief, to the point of fanaticism, both hierarchy and pilgrims are now left with the embarrassment of having revered for five hundred years an image that cannot possibly be that of their 'saviour'. Little wonder at the reluctance of the Cardinal of Turin to make the official pronouncement on October 13th 1988.

With belief so firmly orientated in a single, erroneous direction, the urge to seek alternative answers is virtually non-existent – and yet if this error of philosophy can be cast out, and I concede that it will demand a monumental effort from some, then enlightening answers will surely present themselves.

If the carbon dating analysis is correct, and there is no reason to suggest otherwise, then it must be admitted that the Mandylion and the Shroud were, indeed, two separate relics emanating from eras at least 1,200 years apart. It is to be expected that if there is objection enough to the idea of the phenomenon occurring on one occasion, how much more outcry at the suggestion of it happening twice? Yet, as you have read, there have been instantaneous healings at Lourdes on more than one occasion, not just a single, isolated instance. Poltergeist activity, which emanates from the same mind powers, is prolific enough to be almost commonplace in the annals of psychic phenomena – and it is well known that Uri Geller is not the only person able to bend metal by 'supernatural' means, the others being notably led by Matthew Manning. Other forms of psychic manifestation, such as stigmata, levitation and the rest, are never found to be unique, and never will be. Thus, everything I wrote concerning the Mandylion will remain unaltered by me, with the exception of my analysis of the Royal Arch initiation ceremony, the supreme degree of the Master Masons. I concede that the *secrets* referred to therein apply not to the finding of the long lost Mandylion, but to the Shroud and more particularly to the rediscovery of the *technique* by which the impression on it was produced.

Leaving aside the Fundamentalist point of view and their self-imposed chagrin, our attention must inevitably centre on the true mystery of the Shroud, the manner by which the image was fixed on the cloth.

This problem has caused many an academic heartache, not the least to the Reverend David Sox, at one time Secretary of the British Society of the Shroud of Turin. Mr Sox resigned his position in 1981 after tests by American scientist Dr Walter McCrone revealed iron oxide particles adhering to the linen fabric by means of artists tempera. This seemed to show that the image had been painted on, for iron oxide has been a basic constituent of artists paint for centuries. But other scholars disputed this conclusion, pointing out that in mediaeval times it was common practice for an artist to 'touch up' fading relics. Dr McCrone himself was willing to concede that there could be an original image underneath the particles of paint.

As Ian Wilson has carefully explained, scholarly distrust of the Shroud's authenticity stems mainly from a memorandum drawn up in 1389 by Pierre d'Arcis, Bishop of Troyes, for submission to the Pope. It had come to the attention of the Bishop that canons of the collegiate church at nearby Lirey, a mere twelve miles distant, were exposing for purposes of veneration a cloth which, with papal authorization, they described as a likeness or representation of the 'soudarium' (burial shroud) of Christ. Permission to do so had been obtained from Cardinal de Thury, and not from d'Arcis himself, a move which the Bishop saw as a personal slight. After an investigation, the Bishop wrote to the Pope, giving his opinion that the relic was not the real shroud of our Lord. He had discovered how

> '. . . the said cloth had been cunningly painted, the truth being attested by the artist who painted it, to wit, that it was a work of human skill and not miraculously wrought or bestowed. . . .'

If we recall the reluctance with which the Church authorities eventually embraced the events at Lourdes, doing so as what appears to be a last resort, the integrity and honesty of motive of the Bishop of Troyes will not be above question by any logical investigator. On the other hand, perhaps the 'artist' referred to in the Bishop's memorandum may have been the one who 'touched up' the existing image, if indeed it was painted over.

The enigma of the Shroud image was rendered all the more mystifying on May 28th 1898 when Secondo Pia took the very first photographs of the relic. The outcome stunned all who were there to see, for when the glass negatives began to produce their images in the developer, it could be seen that the pictures were 'positives', as a print should be. For the first time it was realised that the Shroud image is light-reversed, the whole cloth being in the form of a photographic negative. Apparently the conclusions of present day researchers, arrived at after experiments with the most up to date electronic equipment, and which maintain that the image was impressed by a 'burst of radiant energy', may not be far from the truth.

I remind readers that energy at an atomic level can be produced by the trained mind, recalling some pertinent remarks on the subject penned by author Charles Fort, after his own investigation into the saga of John Worrel Keely's 'fuel-less' motor. Fort detailed the story of one Lester J. Hendershot, of Pittsburg, Pennsylvania, as reported in the *New York Herald Tribune*, February 27th and March 10th issues of 1928.

Hendershot had invented a motor which, he claimed, derived its power from 'the earth's magnetic field'. In a test of the invention at Selfridge Field, Detroit, a Major Thomas Lanphier attested to the fact that one small working model of the motor had generated sufficient energy to light two 110 volt lamps, while a second had powered a small sewing machine. The devices themselves weighed only about ten pounds.

It wasn't long before a Dr Frederick Hochstetter, head of his own research laboratory in Pittsburg, went to New York expressly to tell reporters that Hendershot was a fraud. Hochstetter exhibited the motors, demonstrating that he could not produce electric current. You may at this point guess that, as with Keely, the devices responded only to Hendershot himself. The culmination of Hochstetter's exposé was the disclosure that within one of the motors he had discovered a carbon pencil battery. The inventor himself countered the allegations by admitting the presence of the battery, adding that he had noted what had befallen Keely and had placed very little faith in those to whom he had shown the machines. Therefore he had taken the precaution to include in the design several devices, like the battery, which had no other purpose than to deceive anyone attempting to steal the idea. The arguments raged back and forth, although as Fort pointed out, everyone seemed to ignore the fact that a small pencil battery would be totally incapable of powering two 110 volt lamps.

The story of Lester Hendershot ended in a bizarre and, for us, highly significant fashion. Two weeks after the newspaper releases, Hendershot was reportedly admitted to the Emergency Hospital in Washington D.C. He had been demonstrating his motor in the office of a patent attorney, when a bolt of energy, estimated by some at 2,000 volts, shot from it and temporarily paralyzed him. I leave the theosophists to nod understandingly over that item of information.

Readers familiar with the work of Charles Fort will know that he began his investigation of strange reports such as this in the early years of this century, his first volume, *The Book of the Damned*, being published in 1919. There followed *New Lands* (1923), *Lo!* (1932), and finally *Wild Talents* (1932). Interestingly, it was in the latter that he began to cautiously express some obviously re-aligned beliefs.

Page 161
'The function of God is the focus. An intense mental state is impossible, unless there be something, or the illusion of something, to center upon. Given any other equally serviceable concentration-device, prayers are unnecessary. I conceive of the magic of prayers. I conceive of the magic of blasphemies. There is witchcraft in religion: there may be witchcraft in atheism.'

Page 179
'In such a matter as a fright turning hair gray, it is probable that conventional scientists mechanically, unintelligently or with little consciousness of the whyness of their opposition, deny the occurrences, as unquestioning obediences to Taboo. My own concatenation of thoughts is – that, if one's mental state can affect the color of one's hair, a mental state may in other ways affect one's body – and then that one's mental state may affect the bodies of others – and this is the path to witchcraft.'

Thus, after several years of concentrated, investigative thought, Fort came gradually to discard natural prejudice against the concept of mind powers. The Fundamentalists, who believe only what they are told right from the very start, cannot hope to gain the same insight without a similar personal effort. This present volume is offered as a guide towards an alternative point of view, the power of Belief having been shown to be active in many unsuspected spheres. If a 'miracle' transformation of human bodily matter can take place in an instant at Lourdes, or be inflicted on a St Francis of Assisi, cannot the same power affect the atoms of a piece of cloth?

In respect of these mind powers and their possible application in the case of the Shroud, some recent experiments have yielded results which may serve to break down established prejudice and steer the enquiring mind in the right direction, and for the benefit of those who are interested, I offer a brief look at them.

I hardly need state that scientific opinion about the manner in which the Shroud image was impressed is divided and, as yet, unresolved, but it has been generally agreed that the effect was caused by some form of 'scorch', or by a 'burst of radiant energy'. Moreover, the 'scorch' appears to have emanated from within the cloth material, rather than from an outside source, a phenomenon resulting in a partial breakdown of the cellulose fibres of the weave. Another disconcerting fact emerged when the image was analysed by modern computer technicians. Details of the impression were fed into the most sophisticated machines available, resulting in a perfect three-dimensional image, giving the argument that no artist, mediaeval or otherwise, could paint a picture with such an astounding degree of accuracy. The result inferred that such precision could only have been obtained if the cloth actually were wrapped about a body which then emitted some form of energy.

In one recent experiment carried out by the Shirley Institute, a search was made for a material that would break down cellulose in the required manner. Eventually alum was chosen, it having been widely employed by artists of the Middle Ages. Using a pigment called Brazil Wood, a picture was painted on a modern cloth specially woven to duplicate that of the Shroud. It was sized with gum-arabic and, after an ageing process, the finished article was washed – as the Shroud was known to have been at some time in the fifteenth century.

The result was a remarkable comparison, both in image effect and chemical content, with the Shroud itself, and it was judged that the relic could have been produced in this manner – always providing that the artist in question was able to exercise the high degree of accuracy necessary to conform with the computer analysis. Few were willing to agree to the latter possibility.

Closer, perhaps, to the root truth was an experiment conducted by Sister Damien, a Carmelite nun from Salt Lake City, Utah, USA, and her archaeologist colleague, Dr James Strange. After consultation with a local undertaker, Sister Damien discovered a fact little known to lay persons, but accepted by morticians without a second thought – namely that the human body, after death, actually increases its temperature for a short period, sometimes reaching as high as 110 degrees Farenheit. It is assumed that the metabolic process which stabilises the body temperature at its normal 98.6°, ceases immediately upon death, but cellular activity continues for a short while. Ungoverned, this activity induces a post-mortem fever, heating the cadaver before the inevitable cooling process sets in.

As would be expected, Sister Damien accepts the historicity of Jesus Christ without question, and in order to make full use of her newly discovered knowledge, decided to go to Jerusalem itself, there to re-enact the circumstances which she believes took place after the Crucifixion. With fellow archaeologist, Dr Strange, she located a cave near the old city walls in which the experiment they had prepared could take place. Installing a dummy to substitute for the human body, a post-mortem fever condition was simulated by spraying the dummy with an acid sweat solution and filling its hollow interior with warm water to bring about a temperature of 117 degrees F. Then a cloth was placed over it and it was left for a day to cool naturally in the alkaline environment of the cave. The result was gratifying, an image formed on the cloth by the dehydration of its fibres, and thus chemically comparable with the Shroud, although the image itself lacked the clarity and detail of the real relic. I ask you to note that the most important facet of this experiment was the discovery of post-mortem fever.

Let us move now to St Joseph's Hospice in Merseyside, a shelter founded by Catholic priest, Father Francis O'Leary, to care for chronic and terminally ill patients.

In 1981, a faintly visible but nevertheless permanent image of a body appeared on a nylon mattress cover. It shows a man's outline, just as he died, lying on his back with one hand tucked underneath his buttock. No one can offer a solution to the mystery of how such an image was created. The forty-four year old patient died from cancer of the pancreas during the early hours of the morning. When his body was later removed and the bed stripped, the nurses thought the mark on the mattress cover was a stain and attempted to remove it by scrubbing it with antiseptic. But the imprint remained firmly fixed.

According to Father O'Leary and other witnesses, the patient had been wearing a pyjama jacket, lying on a sheet, and with his head on a pillow – yet the imprint appeared only on the nylon mattress cover beneath. Whatever energy or reaction caused the image, did so by penetrating sheet, pillow and pyjama jacket in the process.

The nylon which covered the mattress was of a particular type and therefore traceable, its surface protected by a thin coating of hard-wearing polyurethane. After a study of the image, textile experts found the coating to be undamaged, and therefore concluded that the imprint must have been caused by something which was able to penetrate the coating and act upon the fibres beneath. Researchers at the Shirley Institute experimented until they successfully produced a similar image, an outline which they think was caused by the acid fluid of the patient's last incontinence. However, such an outline would not form on the nylon test piece whilst a sheet was covering it, which meant that either Father O'Leary and the others were concertedly mistaken when they claim that the patient was lying on a sheet and pillow, or that the patient's outline was formed by some other process. To claim that the acid incontinence, which would be centred about the crutch area of the body, would also extend right up to the head and then pass through pillow and sheet without leaving a stain on them does seem to be beyond rational belief. Far more within reason, is the theory of a post-mortem fever inducing such an image – and it is this concept which prompts an important question; in the circumstances of such a fever, are the physical symptoms accompanied by mental emanations that have so far remained undetected?

Fundamentalists, I remind you, are certainly willing to believe that the deceased Jesus Christ's body emitted an energy which magically imprinted a picture upon the fabric of the Shroud, many holding to this belief in spite of the carbon dating analysis which proves otherwise. Is it so difficult, then, to consider the possibility of a human being not bearing the name 'Jesus Christ' as the catalyst for such phenomena?

In *Hermes Unveiled*, I have already offered the opinion that the Mandylion was produced by an Hermetic initiate (a master of positive thinking) focussing his mind so as to impress the required picture on the cloth, resulting in an image which a 10th century text declares was *'due to sweat, not pigment.'* This could be construed as sweat due to a post-mortem fever, as with the Shroud, if one wishes to ignore the mental possibilities and think in physical terms alone. For those, I will detail an incident which took place in Canada not so long ago.

In the early spring of 1977, Canon Cyrille Labrecque, the Catholic priest who founded the Order of the Adorers Convent at Beauport, Quebec, slipped peacefully away from life at the age of ninety-three. A victim of lung disease, he had been bedridden for many months prior to his demise. After he died, the nuns dressed him for burial, and his shoes, long unused, were taken out of his wardrobe and placed upon his feet. Some time later, it was found that the canon's left leg was raised in the air, due it was thought, to a post-mortem contraction of the muscles which sometimes takes place. But it was at this point that the mourning nuns claimed to be able to see a facial likeness of Christ on the now exposed sole of the canon's left shoe, a likeness somewhat similar to that on the Shroud of Turin. Subsequently, thousands of pilgrims flocked to the convent to see the 'miracle shoe', as it came to be called. Doctor Otto Gubelli, a professor of inorganic chemistry at the Laval University, Quebec, examined the shoe, later stating that

'There is no possibility whatsoever that the face was placed there by a human being using artificial means.'

For those interested, a picture of the shoe was published in Britain by the *Sunday People*, page 5, September 24th edition, 1978.

As I have already indicated, the key to such phenomena lies in the latent powers of the mind brought into play when the subconscious is either wittingly, or unwittingly, activated. If the facial likeness on canon Labrecque's shoe is not judged a 'coincidence', a 'trick of the light', or a deliberate fraud by the convent nuns, then I point out that the canon himself did not have to look like Christ in order for the likeness to be 'miraculously' transferred to the material of the shoe sole. As a devout Catholic, the canon doubtless believed fervently in his concept of Christ – possibly believing also that the imprint on the Turin Shroud was a genuine picture of one whom he had been taught to regard as mankind's saviour. The power of Belief is a tool which will obey the user, whatever his or her convictions.

As Ian Wilson has remarked, other shrouds have survived, from as far back as the ancient Egyptian dynasties, some of which bear a form of imprint, showing that the Egyptian embalmers must have been familiar with the phenomenon of post-mortem fever and *possibly of the mental effects which accompany it.*

I would remind readers also, that certain mediums, when their minds are engaged in producing psychic phenomena which has no religious basis, often experience an increased heart rate and a rise in bodily temperature similar to that of a slight fever – and perhaps similar to that of a post-mortem fever.

Bibliography

Recommended reading for those interested in positive thinking.

Bristol, Claude: *The Magic Of Believing*, Prentice-Hall Inc. New York 1948. Reprinted L.N. Fowler Ltd, London 1959

Clark, Rebecca: *Macro-Mind Power* Parker Pub. Co. 1978. Reprinted A. Thomas & Co, 1980

Coué, Emile: *Self Mastery by Conscious Auto-suggestion*, George Allen & Unwin, 1984

Hall, Manly P.: *Masonic, Hermetic, Cabbalistic & Rosicrucian Symbolical Philosophy*, Philosophical Research Society, 1928

Huxley, Aldous: *The Perennial Philosophy*, Chatto & Windus, 1946. Reprinted 1969

Jung, Carl: *Collected Works*, Vol 12, Routledge & Kegan Paul, 1953

Koran, Al: *Bring Out The Magic In Your Mind*, reprinted A. Thomas & Co, 1972

Levi, Eliphas: *The Great Secret, Doctrine of Transcendental Magic*, Rider & Co.

Maltz, Maxwell, M.D.: *Psycho-Cybernetics*, Prentice-Hall Inc USA, 1960

Peale, Norman Vincent: *The Power Of Positive Thinking*, 1953, World's Work Ltd – Windmill Press

Wallace, Helen Rhodes: *How To Enter The Silence*, Science of Thought Press, reprinted Aquarian Press, 1985